P9-DXI-083

FABIO'S
— 30-MINUTE —
ITALIAN

FABIO'S
—30-MINUTE—
ITALIAN

Over 100 Fabulous, Quick and Easy Recipes

FABIO VIVIANI

St. Martin's Press

New York

www.stmartins.com

Book design by Shubhani Sarkar, sarkardesignstudio.com

Cataloging-in-Publication Data is available from the Library of Congress.

ISBN 9781250109958 (hardcover)

ISBN 9781250109965 (e-book)

Our books may be purchased in bulk for promotional, educational, or
business use. Please contact your local bookseller or the Macmillan
Corporate and Premium Sales Department at 1-800-221-7945, extension
5442, or by e-mail at MacmillanSpecialMarkets@macmillan.com.

First Edition: May 2017

10 9 8 7 6 5 4 3 2 1

To my amazing wife, Ashley, and my son, Gage—
anything I do, wherever I go, any decision I make
is only to make sure that you guys will get the best life (and food)
that I can possibly give you.

This book is dedicated to you both.
Honey, please put it to use sometimes. Just kidding!
I'll cook for you till my last breath.

CONTENTS

ACKNOWLEDGMENTS

Few are the brave who helped me with this "30-minute" journey. To John Paolone, my head of culinary, my chef Johnathan Lynch, and to Bambi Osaka, thanks guys for always making a crapload of dishes so fast and so wonderful that I am able to execute so many recipes in so little time.

To Matt Armendariz, my brother from another mother. Your amazing craft with your camera makes my food even more appealing, and your amazing heart makes every day working with you a pleasure. I love you, man. Without you this wouldn't be such an amazing cookbook.

To Mary Goodbody, my writing partner, because an intelligent person was needed to read over and fix my stupid English. And to the whole team at St. Martin's Press—Elisabeth Dyssegaard, Will Schwalbe, Laura Apperson, and Donna Cherry—for helping make this book a success and selling millions of copies.

To Mike Langner and Michael Psaltis, thanks guys for always bringing good business my way. Keep doing it!

INTRODUCTION

Italian food inspires me like nothing else, and yet you may wonder: Why another book about it? Our culinary heritage is so rich and so varied that I don't think there can be too many good explorations of Italian food. Plus, who doesn't like it? The recipes in this book are for simple, relatively quick dishes that American home cooks will love. I love them! And I now live in the United States with my wife, Ashley, and our young son, Gage, and cook in an American kitchen in Chicago. This means I know without a doubt that each and every one of these recipes works in an American kitchen with ingredients bought in American markets.

This isn't always the case with recipes imported directly from Italy. Italy is a country, of course, but it's really a conglomerate of twenty-one regions, each with its own cuisine, traditions, flavors and local pride. We don't look for what's similar about our cooking; we revel in what's different. You can drive twenty-five or thirty miles in any direction in Italy and find a completely different interpretation of Italian cuisine. To me, this makes my country endlessly interesting but not always easy to explain. I have attempted to simplify some of the food here with appealing recipes without any sacrifice of flavor or authenticity.

HOW ITALIANS EAT

Italians are known to spend a long time at the table—but not a long time in the kitchen. We're always eating but not always cooking, and I hope that with the recipes in this book I will translate some of my Italian originality into your life. I will talk about how we prep food and how we create dishes, and along the way I will showcase some of the things we do really, really fast.

I want to give you the essence of Italy in *Fabio's 30-Minute Italian*. I'm from Tuscany, an area that includes the city of Florence and is overall about the size of greater Los Angeles, and many (though not all) of the dishes included here reflect my heritage. When I prepare a meal, very often the goal is to spend three hours at the table, but not that same amount of time in the kitchen. I, like my country-men, prefer to lay the table with an array of relatively easy dishes from pastas and soups to salads and starters and then invite friends and family to sit down and EAT!

ITALY TO AMERICA

I came to California in the fall of 2005 for a vacation. I was twenty-seven and didn't speak a word of English, but I had recently sold my businesses in Italy and was enjoying having a lot of money in my pocket. I'd had a good deal of success in Italy with restaurants, a dance club and a bed and breakfast, and had visions of sitting on the beach in Malibu, sipping mojitos while I daydreamed about the future. But it was not to be because at about the same time, my dad had a business setback and I had to step in and help my family financially, which set me back pretty much to zero.

I didn't move back to Italy, though. Instead I stayed in California. In those early days, I was astounded by the scale of things in the United States. In Italy, I could buy a pint of milk and a single chicken breast in any food market; here in America everything is sold in large packages. What was I going to do with a gallon of milk? A package of eight chicken breasts? Nowadays I can't imagine getting along without Costco, but at first I didn't know what to do with it. What would I do with thirty-six rolls of toilet paper? But you're lured by the deals, so it's easy to overbuy. And it's why there's so much waste.

One of my first trips to a supermarket in Ventura County in Southern California, where I settled, was a few weeks before Thanksgiving—not that I had ever heard of the holiday. Everywhere I looked I saw turkeys, turkey pans, turkey gravy, frozen turkey, turkey breasts, and turkey stuffing. *Americans really love their turkey*, I thought, and made a mental note to put turkey on the menu of any restaurant where I might work. A few weeks later I returned to the same Whole Foods and there wasn't a turkey in sight. *What's wrong with the people who manage this store?* I wondered. *Don't they know how much Americans like turkey?*

A year later I was working at an Italian restaurant in Ventura. William Shatner was a regular customer, and he and I became friends. When Thanksgiving rolled around he invited me to join him and his family for the meal, saying he was going to deep-fry a turkey in the backyard; I brought along a plump chicken. The actor set his backyard on fire with the hot oil and after we put it out, I roasted the chicken. It was delicious.

It wasn't long before the guy I worked for and I became business partners, found an investor, and opened our first restaurant, Café Firenze. I have now lived in this country for more than ten years, am married and have a son. And not only am I familiar with American supermarkets, I now appreciate them. Italy is my homeland, but these days, America is my home.

COOKING HERE AND IN ITALY

I encourage you to use the freshest food you can find because when it's fresh and you know a simple technique or two for preparing the food, cooking begins to be fun—it goes from being a headache to being a pleasure. Your skill level might not be where you wish it were, but that does not mean you can't create a feast to wow everyone!

When I was growing up, we ate anything that was cheap. We had very few choices about what to cook and eat, but that didn't mean the food wasn't delicious. I learned how to make pasta when I was five or six years old. Why? Making your own pasta wasn't a fancy thing to do; it was a necessity. Flour, eggs and water are less expensive than boxes of pasta, and since we ate pasta once or twice a day, this was important.

I know most of my readers will buy pasta, but that won't stop me from including recipes for it in the book; I even have a recipe for gluten-free pasta. Try it! It's easy and it's fun. Get your kids involved. (Setting me up with a pile of flour and a few eggs to crack into it was how my great-grandmother kept me quiet for long stretches of time when I was a kid!)

Let me tell you another story about my great-grandmother and me. I had a, shall we say, "sparkling" personality when I was a small child—I raced around our house like a madman. It was my wheelchair-using great-grandmother's job to keep me occupied while the rest of the family went to work. Not only did she teach me to make pasta (more about that on page 79), but she positioned me between her knees as we wheeled around the house. I became an extension of her, sort of mimicking Leonardo DiCaprio on the prow of the *Titanic* as I leaned over tables and retrieved items off countertops.

My great-grandmother had a friend who often dropped off a basket of apples from his orchard, knowing how much Grandma liked apple pie, which in Italy is more like a sponge cake. She blended the batter by hand, ignoring her small electric mixer. Instead, she handed me a spoon and told me to keep stirring the batter until all the lumps were gone. Unless you're stupid or five years old, you know a spoon won't take care of lumps—but as a little kid, I kept after them, stirring and stirring. Finally, Grandma said it was time to bake the cake, and once she put it in the oven, she turned to me with her finger on her lips and said, "Shhhhhh! The cake is sleeping in the oven." And so she got me to be quiet for a while. These days you aren't supposed to lie to kids, but back then it was survival! The only way Grandma got a breather.

Everyone in our household worked hard, and so my grandmother and my mother often prepared the evening meal using quick cooking techniques so that we were able to sit down to dinner soon after everyone arrived home. Over the years, I've adapted these techniques for a modern American kitchen equipped with food processors, blenders, large stoves and dishwashers, all of which make cooking easy. I've also included some recipes that require long cooking times but are very easy to assemble, so you can go off and do other things while the food simmers and bubbles its way to being cooked.

HOW TO FIND TIME TO COOK

I've been cooking for more than twenty-seven years and can make just about anything and everything, so you might think I don't "get it" when I say these are simple, fast and easy recipes. But I do. People I meet when I give cooking demos or who approach me in airports tell me that they don't cook because cooking just "takes too long." Believe me, it takes less time to flip a chicken breast a few times in a hot skillet than it does to find the local takeout joint online, choose what you want, and then wait for it to be delivered. And every time you flip that chicken breast and "cook" dinner, your confidence grows.

As I'll explain in greater detail, once you embrace the idea of planning and prepping food ahead of time, you can cook a fantastic meal. If the ingredients are on hand, you can put together a warming soup in the time it takes to boil water (or broth). If you've made meatballs earlier in the month and

frozen them, you can put together an incredible pasta dish within minutes after you pull the meatballs from the freezer (almost!).

HOW MY COOKING CHANGED

I own fourteen restaurants in Chicago, Southern California, and Arizona. These keep me plenty busy. Add to this the television work I do, and you'll understand why I sometimes have trouble catching my breath.

Considering my crazy life, is it surprising I am currently interested in fast, easy cooking? But I have a much better reason for wanting to get food on the table soon after I arrive home for the day.

My son, Gage, was born in the fall of 2015, and since that day, my wife, Ashley, and I have changed our eating habits. We like to eat with the baby, the whole family gathered around the table, so I am always eager to get the meal on the table so we can have this family time. (In case you're wondering, I'm the cook in the family, which makes sense. Would you cook if I lived in the same house? Ashley is an awesome wife and mother; I cook.)

This is how it's done in Italy—the whole family eats together. My son doesn't eat baby food and by the time he was ten months old, he'd eaten his fair share of fresh vegetables and lean protein. I cut up adorable little pieces of pasta, meat and chicken for him. I cook carrots and zucchini so they're soft and then mash them with a fork to puree them. He's tried burrata cheese and loves its creaminess. As I write this, he's starting to explore food very happily, which thrills both Ashley and me. When Gage is three, I want to see him with a chicken leg in his hand, not a can of soda.

HOW TO SAVE TIME IN THE KITCHEN

As you cook or read your way through this book, you'll find that I offer ideas for saving time in the kitchen. I am *not* trying to make cooking painless so that you're in and out in minutes. Just the opposite. I hope you'll try new dishes with simple preparations to make your time in the kitchen joyful and productive—and, when you want it to be, quick and easy.

Anyone who has spent time in my beautiful homeland knows that Italians excel at cooking, but we've also found ways to put together spectacular meals without a lot of fuss. As you spend time cooking in your own kitchen, two things will happen: First, you will enjoy cooking more and more, and second, you will become a better, more confident cook.

Here are few tips for organizing your kitchen so that it fits your style of cooking:

- Assemble tools and other equipment for specific tasks in separate drawers. Use drawer organizers to make it easy to spot the spatula or tongs you need.
- Put a ceramic container near the stove and load it up with your favorite cooking utensils and gadgets.
- Invest in a good set of knives and learn how to keep them sharp. I recommend an eight-inch chef's knife, a small paring knife, and a serrated knife for cakes and breads. This trio will save you time in the kitchen.
- Stock a small tray with frequently used oils, vinegars, herbs, and spices, as well as salt and pepper, and keep it on the counter or in an easy-to-reach cupboard.
- Organize spices on a lazy Susan or other spice organizer. The lazy Susan is my best friend when it comes to accessing spices, which I keep on it with the labels facing out. I also like larger lazy Susans for holding pots and pans that might otherwise wind up at the back of a dark cabinet.
- Clear clutter from kitchen counters daily. Crowded counters make the idea of cooking stressful. Keep mail in a basket and recycle papers you don't need; store large and infrequently used equipment in the pantry or other cabinets; put non-kitchen items where they belong elsewhere in the house.

- Organize cabinets so that you aren't searching constantly for pots, pans, lids, and the like. A big thing for me is an organized "Tupperware" cabinet. All the lids are stored by size and the containers are organized by style and size so that they nest.

Although I promise quick cooking with the recipes that follow, and while most take about half an hour to prepare, this isn't magic. To achieve the thirty-minute goal, I've come up with a few strategies that really work:

- Develop a repertoire of simple-to-prepare recipes. If you are familiar with a few meals that you know your family likes, keep those on file so that you can occasionally take a break from trying something new. You'll enjoy cooking a lot more.
- Plan your meals for the week and shop accordingly. This will save shopping time, and more importantly you won't spend unnecessary time worrying about what to cook for dinner.
- Try not to shop during "rush hour." If you can manage trips to the supermarket before 9 a.m. and after 8 p.m., when traffic is lightest, you will get in and out in record time. If you can't, keep in mind that the busiest times for supermarkets is between 5 p.m. and 7 p.m. and any time on the weekends.
- Buy produce in season. Not only will you save money, you will save time, too, because you don't have to do much with seasonal fruits and veggies to benefit from their full flavors.
- Wash and prep fruits and vegetables when you get home from the market. If you wash and cut up the fruits and veggies that you'll need for the week's meals, you're ahead of the game. Store them in lidded containers, ready to be used at a moment's notice.
- Batch cook whenever you can. This essentially means creating leftovers by doubling

or tripling recipes and then refrigerating or freezing the extra for a meal later in the month.

- Plan freezer meals by spending a little time prepping meals that can be frozen for a month or two. Mark and date the containers and keep them in a designated area of the freezer.

I hope you enjoy the recipes I've chosen to highlight how Italian food can be made quick and easy. I know we all have a few standby meals that we turn to week after week, dishes that we know our family likes and that we can cook without a recipe. I have a number of those "old reliables" myself, but there are always those days when you want something different. Here you go! I hope that after you try a few of the dishes in *Fabio's 30-Minute Italian*, they will join your family's roster of favorites.

NOTES FROM FABIO'S KITCHEN

ON RECIPE BASICS IN THIS BOOK

- Pasta is dried unless otherwise specified.
- All salt is kosher or coarse unless otherwise specified.
- Pepper is always freshly ground black pepper unless otherwise specified.
- All red wine is dry and something you'd be happy drinking. It should not be bad wine or anything labeled as "cooking wine."
- I prefer you use homemade chicken stock, but if you use store-bought, it should be organic and low sodium.
- All dairy products are full fat unless otherwise specified.
- Butter is always unsalted unless otherwise specified.
- Mayonnaise also should be homemade, although nothing will happen to you if you use store-bought.
- All eggs are large unless otherwise specified.
- All flour is all-purpose unless otherwise specified.
- All sugar is white granulated unless otherwise specified.
- The heat intensity for stovetop cooking is always medium unless otherwise specified.
- Plastic bags for marinating and/or storage should be sturdy, and zippered or sealable.

ON KITCHEN GEAR

When it comes to equipping your kitchen for **fast, easy cooking**, I have a few recommendations. First, learn to rely on the slow cooker. I know it sounds a little nuts to use a slow cooker for fast cooking, but it takes only minutes to toss ingredients in the cooker, and then you can walk away for several hours while the food cooks.

Next, I suggest at least one large skillet. In about twenty minutes, you can pan sear just about anything, from chicken and beef to fish and vegetables.

I am not a big fan of blending, but a good blender such as a Vitamix allows you to make vinaigrettes and sauces in seconds. Throw in the vinegar, oil, pepper, garlic, and herbs, and one, two, three, pulse, pulse, pulse! An immersion blender works well, too, to make soups, sauces, even mashed potatoes. You can get a good one for about thirty bucks and you'll use it a lot.

I believe in food processors. They're great. A small one will suffice most times, and you literally will be able to chop onions and garlic in seconds. You'll rarely use a large, four-quart food processor unless you decide to make your own pasta dough. But of course I hope you'll try making pasta, so you might want both sizes.

STARTERS

In Italy we don't really have appetizers, at least not in the way Americans think of them. Sure, we always eat a little something while we're waiting for the main meal, something to go with the wine we've already started drinking and to get us ready for what's to come. This might be cold cuts, cheese, raw vegetables or even pureed white beans (sort of Italian hummus). Or it might be some good bread to dip in softened, flavored butter. Any of these foods are quick to prepare and assemble and can be eaten standing up, which is how we often consume them.

In this chapter, I have recipes for starters that are more in line with American tastes but still very Italian. Some could be doubled or tripled and become a full meal. Others could be paired together to make a light lunch or dinner, or they can stand on their own as tasty preludes to dinner.

Toasted Bruschetta with Fresh Burrata Cheese and Honey-Pickled Shallots

Bruschetta—spoken as though the *ch* is a *k*—means "toasted" in Italy. And so, while it's nothing more exotic than toast, you can serve it with so many things it quickly becomes special. When I was a kid, we didn't have much money or food, and even bread on the table was cause for celebration. Ever since, I've always appreciated good bread. Toasted it's even better. Here I combine it with a tomato sauce and a wonderful cheese called burrata. Now common in the United States, burrata is the creamy, sweet curds of mozzarella with a high fat content. My grandfather made a similar cheese in Italy that was better, but a good store-bought burrata comes close. The pickled shallots shouldn't worry anyone—they're pickles for beginners. I like them because they add acidity to all sorts of dishes, although here the honey smooths them out a little. Make them and let them live in your refrigerator to serve here and also with steak, burgers, and other cheeses.

Serves 2 to 4

2 TO 3 HOURS
12 MINUTES ACTIVE TIME

4 small shallots

3 tablespoons honey

2 tablespoons white balsamic vinegar

1 tablespoon water

1 star anise

1 small loaf of ciabatta bread

1 cup seeded, diced Roma tomato

10 leaves basil, chopped

10 black olives, sliced

8 ounces burrata cheese

Fresh basil, torn

Grana Padano cheese, grated, for garnish

Olive oil, for brushing

Salt and pepper

1. Peel the shallots and cut them into thin slices using a mandoline or sharp knife. Combine them in a plastic bag with honey, vinegar, water and star anise. Let this sit for 2 to 3 hours to pickle.

2. Preheat the broiler to high. Cut the ciabatta bread in half horizontally, brush with olive oil, place on a sheet tray into the oven, and toast lightly.

3. In a bowl, mix together tomato, chopped basil, olives and pickled shallots. Set aside.

4. Arrange the burrata over the bread; season with salt and pepper to taste. Scoop the tomato mixture on top and garnish with fresh torn basil and Grana Padano cheese.

Roasted Garlic, Ricotta and Herb-Marinated Shrimp Tarts

This is a showstopper, the perfect appetizer to make when you want to impress your neighbor or the boss. Yet it's simple to assemble and incredibly tasty. I always have frozen puff pastry in the house, which makes this extra easy. I never make my own puff pastry—too much work, and the store-bought is just as good. There is no one brand I endorse; try a few and find your favorite.

Serves 6 to 8

15 MINUTES PREP TIME
20 MINUTES COOKING TIME

1 package puff pastry
sheet, thawed

2 eggs, beaten and divided

½ cup grated Grana Padano
cheese, divided

4 cloves garlic, sliced

1 pound peeled and deveined,
tail-on shrimp, 21–25 ct.

2 tablespoons
extra-virgin olive oil

¼ cup chopped tarragon

½ cup chopped parsley

1 pound ricotta cheese

Torn parsley leaves,
for garnish

Olive oil, for frying

Salt and pepper

1. Preheat oven to 350°. Unfold the pastry sheet, pinching seams together if necessary, and place onto a sheet tray. Brush with half the egg wash. Prick the pastry sheet all over with a fork.

2. Sprinkle half of the Grana Padano cheese on puff pastry; place the sheet tray on the lower rack of the oven. Bake for 3 to 5 minutes or until cheese forms a light crust. Let cool for 3 minutes.

3. While cooking and cooling puff pastry, grab a large skillet and heat to medium high. Drizzle in a touch of olive oil and add garlic, shrimp, salt and pepper. Cook for 1 minute, then pull off the heat and let cool.

4. Combine the olive oil, tarragon, parsley, remaining egg, and ricotta cheese in a bowl. Mix thoroughly and spread over puff pastry, then position cooled shrimp and garlic on top. Season to taste.

5. Toss back in the oven to finish cooking for 15–20 minutes, or until golden brown.

6. Garnish with remaining Grana Padano cheese and parsley leaves.

FABIO SAYS

If your hands smell after chopping or slicing **garlic or onions**, rub them with a stainless steel spoon or a dull knife and then wash them with warm water and soap. Or, roll a small handful of coffee beans around in your hands to remove the odor.

Mascarpone and Ricotta–Stuffed Peaches with Basil and Aged Balsamic

Everyone loves peaches in season, and when you remove the pits and fill the fruit with a rich cheese filling they become a plated first course (or even dessert). My wife walks around the house eating them out of her hand, but I like them on a plate. I also like to roast them at 375°F for about 5 minutes, already halved and filled with the cheese. This is especially beneficial when peaches are not quite as juicy as they are at the peak of their season.

Serves 4 to 6

10 MINUTES PREP TIME
5 MINUTES ASSEMBLY TIME

1 teaspoon salt

1 teaspoon pepper

1 tablespoon honey

¼ cup cream cheese, softened

½ cup ricotta cheese

¾ cup mascarpone cheese

4 ripe peaches, cut in half, pits removed

10 basil leaves, torn

Aged balsamic glaze*, as desired

Extra virgin olive oil, as desired

Combine salt, pepper, honey, cream cheese, ricotta cheese and mascarpone cheese in a bowl and mix completely. Scoop mixture on top of peach halves, scatter torn basil on top and drizzle as you see fit with balsamic glaze and extra virgin olive oil.

* Balsamic glaze is basically a reduced balsamic vinegar with the addition of honey. Put 4 cups balsamic in a saucepan on medium heat. Cook until reduced by half, then add 1 cup of honey. You can put it in a squeeze bottle and store it in the fridge.

Peaches and Prosciutto di Parma Puff Pastry Tarts

Looking for a nice appetizer or even a light meal? Here you go. If you have packaged puff pastry in the freezer, the rest of the ingredients just fall into place: juicy, ripe peaches, creamy mascarpone, a few slices of salty prosciutto and then a drizzle of honey for a touch of sweetness. This is somewhat similar to the Mascarpone and Ricotta Stuffed Peaches on page 8—but why not? I love peaches!

Serves 4

10 MINUTES PREP TIME
20 MINUTES COOKING TIME

Flour for dusting

½ package
puff pastry, thawed

¼ cup honey

¾ cup mascarpone cheese

¼ cup softened cream cheese

3 peaches, pitted and cut into thin wedges

10–12 slices prosciutto di Parma

½ cup grated Grana Padano cheese

1. Preheat oven to 350°F.

2. Sprinkle a surface with a little flour and roll out the puff pastry into a rectangle.

3. Use a fork to press the sides of the puff pastry down to create a crimped pattern. Then place on a sheet tray.

4. Combine the honey, mascarpone cheese and cream cheese in a bowl and spread over the pastry. Lay peaches all over pastry. Place in the oven to cook 12–14 minutes, or until the edges are golden brown.

5. Cut into pieces and top with prosciutto and Grana Padano. Serve right away.

Baked Gruyere, Grana Padano and Caramelized Onion Tart

I'm a big fan of baked cheese, and this tart is delicious: gooey, melting cheese with caramelized onions. I love all tarts, and whenever you bake one anything you put on top of it is special. This one will be a showstopper sitting in the middle of your table.

Serves 6 to 8

10 MINUTES PREP TIME
30 MINUTES COOKING TIME

2 tablespoons olive oil

6 tablespoons butter

2 pounds red and white onions, sliced

5 cloves garlic, sliced

½ cup heavy cream

⅔ cup balsamic vinegar

3 eggs

1 cup grated Gruyere cheese

2 15-cm store-bought pie shells, baked

1 ¼ cup grated Grana Padano cheese

Salt and pepper

1. Preheat oven to 375º F. In a large sauté pan, add the oil and butter. Once it starts to bubble, add onions and garlic. Stir and cook until well caramelized.

2. Add the cream and balsamic vinegar. Reduce until onions are completely coated, about 6 to 8 minutes. Once it resembles syrup, remove and set aside.

3. Beat eggs, and mix in the Gruyere cheese and onions. Season to taste with salt and pepper. Divide evenly between the two pie shells.

4. Place on baking sheets, sprinkle with the Grana Padano, and toss in the oven. Cook for 15–20 minutes, or until filling is set and starting to brown.

FABIO SAYS

I chop, grind or "press" about five pounds of **garlic** every six months or so. I then freeze tablespoon amounts in tiny plastic bags. This means I have more than a hundred small bags of chopped garlic ready to go at any time. You might not need as much garlic, but even eight or ten tablespoons will make life easier. Next time you're chopping one clove, chop four or five more cloves to stash in the freezer. It might be easier to put them through a garlic press—just fine. Also, check out the Roasted Garlic recipe on page 255. Prepping garlic in the way that I suggest here may be easier than chopping all those cloves. Either way, you've got garlic-to-go.

Crispy Fried Summer Squash Blossoms

My wife loves these. For her, they are the ultimate starter, side dish or snack, and I think she would eat them three times a day if I made them. Wait, amend that: I *know* she would! Do squash blossoms fall in the category of vegetables? They're flowers that eventually turn into squash—unless Ashley picks them first and convinces me to fry them up. I am with her on this. These are delicious!

Serves 4 to 6

10 MINUTES PREP TIME
25 MINUTES COOKING TIME

20 squash blossoms
2 cups sparkling water
2 cups flour
2 cups light oil
Salt and pepper

1. Keep the flowers in sparkling water for about 30 minutes, then pull them out. Without patting them dry, toss them all over with the flour in a bowl. Let them sit in the flour for at least 15 minutes.

2. Place the flowers on a wire rack. Heat the oil to 385°F in a cast-iron pan, and cook them till crispy to the touch on all sides, about 2 minutes.

3. Season with salt and pepper.

FABIO SAYS

Americans might think **frittatas** are for breakfast, but in Italy they are most often eaten for lunch or dinner, or even as a snack. When I was growing up in Florence, Italy, and we lived with my grandparents and great-grandmother, we ate eggs for dinner nearly every night. My grandfather kept chickens in a coop near the garden where he grew vegetables for us. It was a distance from our apartment, so he got in the habit of collecting the eggs on the way home from work. As soon as he walked through the door, my grandmother started cooking, very often making a frittata with whatever else was in the house: tomatoes, spinach, cheese. We didn't have much, and those eggs sustained us.

Italians like frittatas on bread as a sandwich and tend to think of them as sort of a "kitchen sink" kind of dish—almost anything goes: meat, vegetables, cheese, herbs. I always include cheese because it creates a moist environment—with cheese, even a beginner won't end up with a dry frittata with overcooked eggs (or if they do, the frittata will still be tasty). You can eat the two frittatas on the following pages for breakfast or brunch, or serve them as an appetizer or snack. In Italy, we don't really eat breakfast. There are no hash browns, bagels or cream cheese and lox. Once we're up, we don't take time for more than cappuccino and a croissant. No one cooks in the morning!

Frittatas differ from omelets. Omelets are French and are more complicated than their Italian cousins. They need a special pan and are folded so they slide from the pan. Nothing like that for frittatas. If you can crack an egg, you can make a frittata.

Frittata with Prosciutto di Parma, Sausage, Red Onions and Butter Shallots

This frittata, made with spicy sausage, prosciutto and mozzarella, is pure Italian. Serve this for lunch, dinner, a snack, or after a midnight raid on the refrigerator. It's easy and quick once you gather the ingredients.

Serves 4

10 MINUTES PREP TIME
20 MINUTES COOKING TIME

1 tablespoon dried thyme

3 tablespoons half-and-half

10 eggs

1 tablespoon olive oil

5 tablespoons butter

½ cup shaved red onions

2 shallots, sliced

½ cup crumbled spicy Italian sausage

3 ounces finely diced prosciutto

½ cup fresh mozzarella cheese, torn

¼ cup minced Italian parsley

Salt and pepper

1. Preheat oven to 375°F.

2. Beat the thyme, half-and-half and eggs together in a bowl, and season with salt and pepper.

3. Melt the olive oil and butter in a 12-inch oven-safe nonstick skillet over medium heat until foaming. Stir in the red onion and shallots. Season with salt and pepper and cook for 5 minutes, then add the sausage and prosciutto. Cook for 2 minutes and add eggs. Stir gently until ⅓ of the egg is set.

4. Place the cheese evenly in the eggs and transfer to oven. Cook until just set, about 8–10 minutes. Remove and scatter the parsley to garnish.

Creamy Montasio and Prosciutto Frittata with Chives and Parsley

Made simply with cheese, meat and herbs, this frittata is full-flavored and delicious. I think Montasio cheese—a creamy cow's milk cheese that's wildly popular in Italy and just establishing a foothold in the United States—is the perfect frittata cheese. It melts beautifully and provides not only great flavor but perfect texture as well.

Serves 2 to 3

10 MINUTES PREP TIME
8 TO 10 MINUTES COOKING TIME

2 tablespoons minced chives

2 tablespoons minced Italian parsley

2 tablespoons whole milk

6 eggs

2 tablespoons butter

2 tablespoons olive oil

⅓ cup Montasio cheese, grated

6 thin slices prosciutto

¼ cup arugula, for garnish

Salt and pepper

1. Preheat the broiler to low.

2. Beat the chives, parsley, whole milk and eggs together. Season with salt and pepper, then heat the butter and oil in a large omelet pan on medium high heat.

3. When the fats have melted, pour in the egg mixture and allow to set for about 1 minute, then pull the edges from the outside to the inside of the pan. This allows the cooked egg to transfer to the middle, while the uncooked egg spreads to the outer edges.

4. When the egg is ¾ cooked, about 2 more minutes, add cheese in small piles around the egg and turn off the heat. Place under the broiler and let cook until cheese melts.

5. Remove and garnish with prosciutto and arugula.

FABIO SAYS

A pinch of salt in the **milk** carton keeps the milk fresh for a few extra days. If you tend to go through milk fairly quickly, there's no need for the salt, but if you don't it will help. Just a pinch! No one wants salty milk.

Americans love salads and create truly impressive ones. They can be the main course or a side dish, and they are the perfect escape when you're in the mood for a modest meal. When it comes to other sides, Americans do pretty well, too, but I don't think anyone in the world cooks vegetables as well as Italians. In this chapter I've teamed salads and sides, knowing that you, like Ashley and me, sometimes make a meal of one or the other or both.

This attitude is different from how I was raised. Salad was always a very simple side dish and, to be honest, we didn't have it often. I don't remember my mom *ever* coming home with a sack of tomatoes and a bag of butter lettuce. When it came to vegetables, we ate what my grandfather grew. Period. End of story.

Throughout Italy this is pretty much the case. Salads usually are humble dishes dressed with nothing more than extra virgin olive oil, red wine vinegar, and salt and pepper. I still like that kind of simplicity, but I've also embraced the American style of making substantial salads—but always with very Italian accents.

Sides are a little different. We love vegetables in Italy and generally eat them when they are in season because that's when they are at their best. We often don't differentiate between a side dish and a main course. A platter of Red Quinoa and Heirloom Carrot Salad with Roasted Grape Tomato Vinaigrette is likely to get equal billing on the dinner table with a platter holding roasted chicken or braised beef. We might eat Ricotta and Sausage Stuffed Tomatoes as a light lunch, or it might be an accent for a more substantial meal. Regardless of how you view these dishes, they make it easy, delicious and exciting to eat your vegetables!

Pasta Salad with Prosciutto di Parma, Roasted Artichoke and Grana Padano Cheese

When my mom makes a pasta salad everyone flips out—they're so good—and because I learned from her, mine are equally mind blowing (I hope!). They're full-on dishes that are welcome as a main course or as a side. That's because I include veggies and protein along with the perfectly cooked pasta, all layered with flavor upon flavor, like a well-composed dish. And as tasty as this is cold or at room temperature, if you like your pasta warm, just heat the salad for about 2 minutes in the microwave.

Serves 4

15 MINUTES PREP TIME
15 MINUTES COOKING TIME

1 ½ cups canned artichoke hearts, halved and patted dry

½ teaspoon red chili flakes

¼ cup chopped basil

¼ cup thinly sliced red onion

½ cup chopped Kalamata olives

½ cup fresh Italian parsley

½ cup grated Grana Padano cheese

½ cup olive oil

½ cup ricotta cheese

½ cup roasted red peppers

2 tablespoons red wine vinegar

2 tablespoons capers

½ cup arugula

8 slices torn prosciutto di Parma

1 pound penne, cooked al dente

Olive oil

Salt and pepper

1. Preheat oven to 425°F.

2. Evenly space the artichoke hearts on a sheet tray. Drizzle with olive oil and season with salt and pepper. Place inside the oven and cook for 10 minutes, or until charred on the edges.

3. Remove from the oven and cut into smaller pieces.

4. In a large bowl, combine the red chili flakes, basil, onion, Kalamata olives, parsley, Grana Padano, olive oil, ricotta, red peppers, red wine vinegar, capers, arugula, prosciutto and penne. Season with salt and pepper and toss to coat.

5. Place pasta salad in a large serving bowl and serve at room temperature or slightly chilled.

Fresh Bean Salad with Roasted Chickpeas, Crispy Mortadella Bites and Mustard Vinaigrette

The whole point of a salad is that just about anything goes, and the trick is to find ingredients that complement each other. You can have a beef salad, a chicken salad or one, like this, that is heavy on the veggies and legumes with a perfect balance of textures and flavors. The diced mortadella—that deliciously fatty Italian sausage—is cooked until it's crispy and then paired with crunchy beans for a rich, meaty accent. I combine canned beans with fresh beans along with the meat, peppers and greens. The lettuce wilts a little under the weight of the dressing and other ingredients, but that's what's supposed to happen. I almost always have a mustard vinaigrette in my fridge, in a spouted bottle that makes it easy to use. As perfect as it is on this salad I like it drizzled over steamed vegetables, grilled fish and chicken too.

Serves 3 to 4

10 MINUTES PREP TIME
20 MINUTES COOKING TIME

FOR THE DRESSING:

2 tablespoons
whole grain mustard

¼ cup red wine vinegar

⅔ cup olive oil

FOR THE SALAD:

1 cup diced mortadella

1 tablespoon minced
Fresno chili pepper

½ cup rinsed chickpeas

½ cup fresh green beans,
blanched, cut on bias

½ cup cannellini beans,
rinsed

½ cup thinly sliced
red bell pepper

1 shallot, sliced thin

2 cups mixed greens

Salt and pepper

Olive oil

1. Take the mustard, red wine vinegar, and olive oil, and place in a blender. Blend on high to combine and season with salt and pepper.

2. In a large saucepan on medium high heat, drizzle in a touch of olive oil and toss in the mortadella. Cook until slightly crispy, about 5–7 minutes, and add the chili and chickpeas. Cook for another 3 minutes and cool on paper towels to absorb excess oil.

3. Place green beans, cannellini beans, bell pepper, shallot, and mixed greens in a large bowl and, once cooled, add the Mortadella mixture. Toss entire mixture with vinaigrette and adjust seasoning with salt and pepper.

Butter Lettuce Salad with Granny Smith Apples, Pomegranate Seeds and Charred Shallot Vinaigrette

Serves 2 to 3

15 MINUTES PREP TIME
10 MINUTES COOK TIME

FOR THE DRESSING:

2 cloves garlic

3 large shallots, peeled and halved

2 teaspoon Dijon mustard

2 teaspoon honey

1 teaspoon chopped thyme

1 cup olive oil

¼ cup red wine vinegar

FOR THE SALAD:

½ head of butter lettuce, hand torn

2 tablespoons pomegranate seeds

½ cup diced Granny Smith apples

½ rib of celery, thinly sliced

Shaved Manchego cheese for garnish

Cracked black pepper

1. To make the dressing, preheat a grill or nonstick pan on medium high heat. Toss the garlic and shallots in a small bowl with a drizzle of olive oil. Place them on whatever hot surface you are using and char the flesh.

2. Place them in a blender with Dijon, honey and thyme and blend on high until well puréed. Place this mixture in a bowl and whisk in the oil and vinegar. Season to taste with salt and pepper. Keep in mind that this is not an emulsified dressing.

3. Place the torn lettuce in a bowl and drizzle the dressing on top. Toss the salad and coat the lettuce. Place the lettuce on your plate and garnish with the pomegranate, apple, celery, and shaved cheese. Finish with cracked black pepper.

Melon, Blood Orange and Prosciutto di San Daniele Salad with Pecorino Dressing

Both the melons and the blood oranges are sweet; the grapefruit is a little bitter. To take advantage of these mixed-up flavors, I pair them with prosciutto, a famous Italian cured meat that is sweeter than similar meats you find in the United States. But the best part of this salad is the dressing. It's made with citrus juices, mustard, olive oil and grated Pecorino cheese. This cow's milk cheese has a noticeable sharpness that makes the dressing sing. I suggest you double, triple, quadruple or ten-fold the dressing and keep it in the fridge or freezer so it's always on hand. It will keep in the refrigerator for a week or two, and for a year frozen in small quantities. Yes. Frozen salad dressing!

Serves 5 to 6

---

20 MINUTES PREP TIME

FOR THE DRESSING:

3 tablespoons olive oil

2 tablespoons orange juice

2 tablespoons Dijon mustard

1 tablespoon lemon juice

2 tablespoons grated pecorino cheese

2 tablespoons chopped Italian parsley

FOR THE SALAD:

1 small honeydew melon, halved

1 small cantaloupe, halved

1 ruby grapefruit

2 blood oranges, or other oranges if not available

8 slices prosciutto di San Daniele, torn into ribbons

1 cup arugula

Mint sprigs, to garnish

Shavings of pecorino, if desired

1. Take melons and scoop out the seeds. Using a melon baller, scoop out as much flesh as possible.

2. Cut the peel and pith from the grapefruit and oranges: Hold the fruit over a bowl to catch the juice, and cut between the membranes to release the segments.

3. To make the dressing: In a blender, take the reserved juices from the citrus, olive oil, orange juice, Dijon mustard, and lemon juice. Blend until smooth. Pour into a bowl and whisk in the cheese and parsley.

4. Arrange the melon pieces, grapefruit and orange segments on four plates. Portion the prosciutto evenly on the plates. Take a little bit of the dressing and spoon over fruit pieces.

5. Take another small amount of dressing and toss with arugula, enough to coat the arugula lightly. Portion the arugula on top of the fruits and prosciutto. Top with mint sprigs. Garnish with shaved pecorino, if desired.

FABIO SAYS ———

These days I am totally into **salad dressings**. I always double the recipe so I have a couple of jars of dressing in the fridge to drizzle over a green salad, sliced tomatoes, a sandwich or grilled chicken—whatever sounds good to me.

Red Quinoa and Heirloom Carrot Salad with Roasted Grape Tomato Vinaigrette

If you can find heirloom carrots that come in an array of colors—purple, red, yellow and orange—and then team them with red quinoa, you'll have a rainbow on your plate that tastes great and is good for you, too.

Serves 4

15 MINUTES PREP TIME
30 MINUTES COOKING TIME

FOR THE VINAIGRETTE:

1 teaspoon Dijon mustard

1 teaspoon honey

1 teaspoon rosemary

1 teaspoon thyme

¼ cup red wine vinegar

1 ½ cup roasted
grape tomatoes

¾ cup light olive oil

¼ cup charred green onion*

Salt and pepper

FOR THE SALAD:

1 red onion, shaved

1 watermelon radish,
sliced paper-thin

4 cups red quinoa,
cooked to manufacturer's
specifications

8 heirloom carrots,
shaved using a peeler

1. In a blender add Dijon, honey, rosemary, thyme, red wine vinegar, and tomatoes. Purée until all ingredients are well incorporated. Slowly drizzle oil into blender to create an emulsion. Add salt and pepper as needed. At the very end add charred onions, and pulse until incorporated but with pieces still visible. Set aside.

2. In a bowl add the onion, radish, quinoa, and carrots. Add the vinaigrette a little at a time, mixing it in gently. Nicely place salad on each plate. Place small drops of vinaigrette around the plate, swoop through each one with a small spoon, and serve.

*To char the green onions, using tongs, hold them 2 or 3 inches above a gas flame, turning until the white and light green parts darken a shade or two. Alternatively, lay the onions in a dry skillet and heat them over medium-high heat, turning, until the onions darken a shade or two. Let the onions cool before chopping and measuring. For ¼ cup, you will need 2 or 3 onions.

Roasted Garden Vegetables with Tangy Lemon Breadcrumbs

Roasting vegetables is an easy way to come up with a fantastic side dish. Choose the root vegetables and others you like, season them with oil and some flavorful ingredients like garlic and basil, and then put them in the oven. For this recipe, I chose fennel, carrots, bell peppers and zucchini, but really, most any vegetables will work. Toss them together and roast until they're caramelized the way you like them, ten, twenty, or thirty minutes.

Serves 6

15 MINUTES PREP TIME
30 MINUTES COOKING TIME

2 tablespoons balsamic glaze, *see note p. 8*

½ cup extra-virgin olive oil

3 teaspoons finely chopped fresh basil

3 teaspoons finely chopped fresh oregano

3 garlic cloves, smashed with a garlic press or pureed with a knife

2 large red onions cut into disks

1 green bell pepper cut into 4 pieces lengthwise, seeds discarded

2 big carrots, quartered lengthwise and cut in half again

3 fennel bulbs, cut in half then quartered

3 zucchini, cut into ⅓-inch-thick rounds

3 tablespoons olive oil

1 cup breadcrumbs

Zest of 2 lemons

Salt and pepper

1. Whisk the glaze and oil in a bowl. Stir in basil, oregano, and garlic. Season to taste with salt and pepper.

2. Preheat oven to 425°F. Toss the onions, bell pepper, carrots, fennel and zucchini into a bowl with the dressing and let sit for about 5 minutes.

3. Toss vegetables once more, transfer into 2 different baking dishes and roast for about 15 to 20 minutes, or until the edges are golden brown.

4. Mix breadcrumbs and lemon zest.

5. Finish with olive oil and the lemon breadcrumbs.

Caramelized Vegetable Capponata with Mint and Lemon

This Italian classic was originally developed to use up tired, old vegetables by mixing them with a sweet-and-sour sauce that masked their odor. I use fresh vegetables here (not any that have been sitting around for days) and dress them with a delicious sauce made from red wine vinegar and brown sugar stirred into marinara sauce. This makes the capponata a delightful side dish or appetizer topping toasted bread.

Serves 4

15 MINUTES PREP TIME
30 MINUTES COOK TIME

1 cup diced carrots

1 cup diced celery

1 large yellow onion, diced small

1 ½ cups olive oil

5 cloves of garlic, crushed

2 tablespoons tomato paste or concentrate

3 large eggplants, skin partially peeled, cut into 1-inch chunks

½ cup capers, drained

½ cup pine nuts

1 ½ cups pitted sliced green olives

4 tablespoons brown sugar

½ cup red wine vinegar

2 cups marinara sauce

1 bunch of basil, stalks removed

1 tablespoon mint

Salt and pepper

Zest of 1 lemon, for garnish

1. In a deep casserole on high heat, prepare the "fondo" with the carrots, celery, onion and olive oil. Cook until the vegetables are nice and caramelized.

2. Add the garlic and half of the tomato paste and cook for another 2 minutes.

3. Add eggplant, making sure that you toss them as they heat up. Keep the fire on high and continue stirring so that they absorb the oil, release their water, and get softer and reduce in size, about 8 minutes.

4. Add the capers, pine nuts and olives and cook another 5 minutes.

5. Add the sugar and vinegar. As soon as the vinegar is reduced, add the marinara sauce mixed with the remaining tomato paste, and cook for another 10 minutes.

6. Add basil and keep reducing on high heat until the marinara is completely reduced and there is no trace of water. Season to taste with salt and pepper.

7. Remove from heat and let rest for about 30 minutes.

8. Serve with mint and lemon zest on top.

Blistered Sweet Pepper and Marinated Feta Salad with Arugula and Quinoa

Quinoa is a superstar. With no gluten yet high in protein, it's a perfect grain. It's also sneaky, making sure it touches just about every ingredient in the salad so that with every forkful you get a sprinkling or more of quinoa. "Hey!" it says, "You can't ignore me!" And who would want to? Here it blends perfectly with honey, dill, fruity olive oil, briny olives, sweet cherry tomatoes, earthy roasted peppers, and creamy, crumbly feta cheese. No one will ever turn feta into a great cheese, but it's a very good cheese that, like quinoa, finds its way into just about every bite so that you can benefit from its salty milkiness. I like this salad as a leftover, and if I make enough, I can happily eat it for three or four days.

Serves 4

10 MINUTES PREP TIME
20 MINUTES COOKING TIME

1 cup red quinoa

1 pound red bell peppers, sliced thin

1 pound yellow bell peppers, sliced thin

¼ cup honey

⅓ cup olive oil

1 pint cherry tomatoes, halved

4 ounces crumbled feta cheese

3 tablespoons chopped dill

¼ cup chopped Italian parsley

¼ cup chopped Kalamata olives

½ cup arugula

Salt and pepper

Olive oil

1. Bring a large pot of water, 2 to 3 quarts, to a boil and add a touch of salt. Pour in quinoa and boil for 6 to 8 minutes. Turn off the heat and let sit for 3 minutes, then drain.

2. While quinoa is cooking, heat a sauté pan on high heat. Add peppers to the pan and cook for 1 minute. Toss and cook for another minute. Turn off the heat and add a touch of olive oil. Season with salt and pepper and toss for 30 seconds. Let sit in the pan for 2 minutes, and then transfer to a plate to cool.

3. Mix the honey and olive oil in a large bowl. Add the tomatoes, feta, dill, parsley, and olives. Toss to combine.

4. Once peppers have cooled to close to room temperature, add to the large bowl along with the arugula and quinoa. Season with salt and pepper and an additional drizzle of olive oil to bring everything together.

Butter Lettuce Salad with Grilled Peaches, Shaved Red Onion, Burrata, Speck and Sherry Vinaigrette

Serves 2 to 4

15 MINUTES PREP TIME
20 MINUTES COOK TIME

1 head of butter lettuce
1 tablespoon Dijon
1 tablespoon honey
¼ cup sherry vinegar
1 small shallot
2 garlic cloves
1 cup extra light olive oil
2 peaches
12 pieces thinly sliced speck
4 2-ounce burrata balls
1 red onion, thinly sliced
Salt and pepper

1. Cut butter lettuce at the base and separate each leaf. Run under water and dry to clean.

2. To make the sherry vinaigrette, place Dijon, honey, sherry vinegar, shallot, garlic cloves and a pinch of salt and pepper into blender. Blend on high for 30 seconds and the slowly pour in extra light olive oil. Finished product should be emulsified. Taste and season with salt and pepper.

3. Preheat a grill pan on medium high heat. Cut peaches in half and remove pit. Cut each half into an additional 4 wedges; brush with oil, salt and pepper. Grill until there are defined grill marks; remove from heat.

4. Take a par-frozen slab of speck and place on slicer. Thinly slice to transparency. Taste speck; it should not be chewy or hard to eat. If this happens, slice even thinner, like prosciutto. If you have no slicer, speck should be available at your local deli.

5. Remove the burrata from the bag and cut each ball into three equal pieces.

6. Take butter lettuce, around 4 pieces, and toss in vinaigrette with red onion and lay on the plate. Drape 3 slices of speck around plate and lettuce. Place three pieces of burrata and 4 wedges of peach around each plate. Season with fleur de sel and crushed black pepper.

Garlic and Honey–Marinated Avocado, Mango and Roasted Chicken Salad

Here's something really nice to do with leftover chicken or turkey, but if you don't have it on hand—and don't feel like roasting a chicken to create "leftovers"—buy a rotisserie chicken from the supermarket. The salad is also good with leftover pork. Here I make enough for four for lunch or a light supper, but if you want to feed larger numbers, double or triple the recipe. It's easy and so good with a grilling menu. I love mayo, but it's overused, especially in the summer, and so here I rely on avocados for silky smoothness.

Serves 4

10 MINUTES PREP TIME
20 MINUTES COOKING TIME

¼ cup honey

2 cloves garlic, grated

2 ripe avocados, peeled, pitted and cut into large cubes

3 tablespoons fresh lime juice

½ cup baby kale

½ cup baby spinach

½ cup mixed greens

½ cup olive oil

1 cup shredded roasted chicken*

1 ripe mango, peeled, pitted and diced

1 large orange, pith removed, divided in segments

1 shallot, thinly sliced

Salt and pepper

1. Toss the honey, garlic and avocados together to coat the avocado.

2. Combine the lime juice, kale, spinach, mixed greens, olive oil, chicken, mango, orange and shallot in a large bowl until dressed. When dressed, add marinated avocado, season with salt and pepper to taste, and toss until just combined.

* As a side note, you can use leftover turkey, game hen, or pork with this recipe for a fast and easy substitution.

Grilled Calamari and Warm Spinach Salad with Orange Segments

If you can't get good quality fresh calamari, frozen does fine. It works for sure in this salad, which is fresh, summery and great for grilling. Let the calamari soak in the simple olive oil and lemon juice marinade while you prep the spinach, but don't leave it longer than fifteen minutes or the lemon will start to "cook" the squid.

Serves 3 to 4

15 MINUTES PREP TIME
20 MINUTES COOKING TIME

12 cleaned calamari
with the inner bone removed

1 teaspoon garlic powder

2 tablespoons
minced Italian parsley

½ cup olive oil

2 lemons, juiced and zested

2 navel oranges

3 cups baby spinach

2 cloves garlic, minced

Salt and pepper

Olive oil

1. Preheat a grill to high heat and clean with a grill brush so that grill marks will really be apparent.

2. Combine calamari bodies and tentacles with garlic powder, parsley, olive oil, and lemon juice and zest. Marinate for 15 minutes.

3. While the calamari sits, supreme the oranges: Using a sharp knife, trim the top and bottom of the fruit. Placing one flat end on a cutting surface, carefully remove the remaining peel and pith and then hold over a bowl. Cut out the individual segments and place them in the bowl. Toss in the spinach and garlic.

4. Heat a sauté pan on medium high heat and add a touch of olive oil. Add the spinach mixture to the pan, season with salt and pepper, and cook for 1 minute. Shake the pan to move everything around, turn off the heat, and cover with a lid.

5. Take calamari bodies and place on the grill with a press on top so that they don't puff up. Cook for 1 minute. Flip and cook another minute in the same fashion. Baste the calamari with the marinade and toss the tentacles on the grill and cook for 30 seconds or so.

6. Serve calamari with warm spinach salad.

Italian Sweet Sausage with Charred Serrano Pepper Potato Salad

Here's a classic, mayonnaise-based potato salad interpreted by me. It's got sausage, chilies, and a hint of horseradish to offset the mustard—all flavors that like each other. I cook everything for this salad on the grill, including the potatoes, which I cook in salted water heated in a saucepan on the grill. You might choose to cook them on the stovetop instead, which is just fine.

Serves 4 to 6

15 MINUTES PREP TIME
30 MINUTES COOKING TIME

2 pounds baby red potatoes

6 Italian sausage links, spicy or mild

4 Serrano chilies

1 teaspoon prepared horseradish

2 tablespoons chopped parsley

2 tablespoons white balsamic vinegar

¼ cup minced chives

⅓ cup stone ground mustard

⅔ cup mayonnaise, store-bought or homemade

1 shallot, shaved on a mandoline

2 green onions, sliced thin on the bias

Salt and pepper

1. Preheat a grill to high and place potatoes in a pot of salted water. Bring the potatoes to a boil and cook until a knife can be inserted and pulls out clean. Take out of the water and set aside to cool off.

2. Make sure the grates are very clean for the best grill marks. Once the grill is hot, place the sausages and chilies on it. Cook the sausages until charred on all sides or until juices run clear. For the chilies, cook until charred to your liking, about 6–8 minutes. Cut chilies into small chunks.

3. For the potato salad, once cooled off, cut potatoes into quarters or sixths depending on their size. Take horseradish, parsley, white balsamic vinegar, chives, mustard, mayo, shallots, green onions and chilies and place in a bowl with potatoes. Mix and season with salt and pepper.

4. Serve sausages on top of potato salad.

FABIO SAYS

Before you chop **hot chilies**, rub a little vegetable oil on your hands to protect them from the spicy chili oil that will be released. This makes your hands slippery, so use the oil strategically. And keep your hands away from your eyes and your mouth.

Ricotta and Sausage–Stuffed Tomatoes

This bold little dish can be a starter, side or a main. Take your pick, but don't neglect to make it. Start with firm tomatoes that will stand up to being stuffed, and when you fill the scooped-out halves, make a nice dome with the filling. I like sweet Italian sausage for this, but you can go with your favorite sausage. When I was young and living in Italy, my grandfather and I sometimes made this with green tomatoes, which were always cheaper than fully ripe ones. We also fried the green tomatoes. Delicious!

Serves 4

15 MINUTES PREP TIME
15 MINUTES COOKING TIME

4 beefsteak tomatoes, cut in half and slightly scooped out

4 tablespoons olive oil

¼ cup chopped parsley

¼ cup julienned sun-dried tomatoes

½ cup chopped Kalamata olives

1 cup grated Grana Padano cheese

1 cup ricotta cheese

¼ pound chopped soppressata

¼ pound cooked sweet Italian sausage

15 basil leaves, roughly chopped

Salt and pepper

Cooking spray

1. Preheat oven to 375°F.

2. Set tomatoes on a sheet tray sprayed with cooking spray. Combine the olive oil, parsley, sun-dried tomatoes, olives, Grana Padano cheese, ricotta cheese, soppressata, Italian sausage and basil in a large bowl and season with salt and pepper. Fill each tomato with an equal amount of the mixture.

3. Place into the oven and cook for 8–10 minutes. Turn off the oven and set the broiler on high. Crust the top for another 2–3 minutes and remove. Let cool slightly and enjoy.

FABIO SAYS

If you have wrinkled, **overripe tomatoes**, it's easy to rejuvenate them. Submerge them in a bowl of cold water with a pinch of salt and let them sit overnight in the refrigerator. They will be firm and smooth when you remove them, but should be used pretty much right away. Like Cinderella's coach, they're only good until midnight!

Roasted Cauliflower Gratin
with Montasio Cheese, Pine Nuts and Bread

Although I have made this with cheddar cheese, it's even better with rich, creamy Montasio. This cow's milk cheese has been made in northern Italy for hundreds of years, but only recently found a foothold in America. I use it to make this gratin with cauliflower instead of potatoes (you could use potatoes, of course, and turn this into "gratin on steroids"). Cauliflower calms down and absorbs any excess moisture in the sauce to leave it smooth and creamy. You can make this extra quickly if you happen to have some blanched cauliflower florets in the freezer.

Serves 4

10 MINUTES PREP TIME
20 MINUTES COOKING TIME

2 pounds cauliflower florets, halved

¼ cup pine nuts

½ cup chopped Italian parsley

½ cup Grana Padano cheese, grated

2 tablespoons Dijon mustard

1 cup mayonnaise, store bought or homemade

1 cup Montasio cheese (if not available use Asiago)

2 cloves garlic, grated

4 green onions, sliced

1 teaspoon dried oregano

1 teaspoon garlic powder

1 teaspoon onion powder

¼ cup panko breadcrumbs

Salt and pepper

1. Preheat oven to 400°F.

2. Bring a pot of salted water to a boil, then drop in the cauliflower. Cook this right below a boil for 5 minutes, then remove the cauliflower and shock it in a large bowl of ice water.

3. Once cooled, arrange the cauliflower in a greased casserole dish evenly. Mix pine nuts, parsley, Grana Padano, Dijon mustard, mayo, Montasio, garlic and onion in a large bowl, season with salt and pepper, and spoon on top of cauliflower. Spread the mixture evenly.

4. Mix the oregano, garlic powder, onion powder, and panko. Spread on top of casserole. Place into the oven and bake for 10–15 minutes until top is golden brown.

Crispy Chickpea, Burrata and Frisee Salad

A great autumn salad made with ingredients you may already have on hand. Well, probably not the burrata, but the creamy cheese is so good, you won't mind a trip to the store!

Serves 4

10 MINUTES PREP TIME

15 MINUTES COOK TIME

1 tablespoon fresh chopped thyme

2 cups chickpeas, drained and rinsed

Zest of two lemons

12 sun-dried tomatoes, store bought or your favorite homemade

1 pound fresh burrata cheese

1 teaspoon Dijon mustard

2 tablespoons apple cider vinegar

½ cup olive oil

1 cup baby arugula

2 cups mixed greens

2 heads of frisee, washed, cleaned, and torn

Salt and pepper

1. Preheat an oven to 400°F. In a bowl, toss together thyme, chickpeas, and lemon zest. Season with salt and pepper and spread on a sheet tray. Place in the oven to cook for 10–15 minutes, or until lightly browned.

2. Arrange the tomatoes and cheese evenly on plates.

3. In a large bowl, combine Dijon mustard, vinegar, olive oil, arugula, mixed greens and frisee. Season with salt and pepper.

4. Remove chickpeas and cool slightly. Toss chickpeas in salad mixture and serve with tomatoes and burrata.

SOUPS

As I have with salads, I've bought into America's love affair with soup. Italians make soup, but we have four or five staples and stick to them. Bread soup, minestrone, pasta e fagioli, maybe a mushroom or white bean soup now and then. Our traditional soups are earthy and wintry and rely on ingredients available in the cold months: beans, root vegetables, hearty greens. We don't eat cold soups or seafood chowders in the summer. That said, we also always say that anything that's cooked can be mixed with chicken stock and heavy cream and turned into a soup, as long as the food is not burned. Italian cooks are happily confident.

The variety of soups featured here are meant to be quick, flavorful and full of familiar Italian flavors and textures. But they're not *really* Italian soups!

Oven-Roasted Pea Soup
with Mint and Mascarpone Dressing

This isn't the split-pea type of pea soup but instead is made with fresh or frozen English peas—those bright green orbs—and then topped with a decadent dollop of mascarpone cheese mixed with cream cheese, which is the Italian answer to crème fraîche or sour cream, but better! Mint and peas are good partners but you don't find mint soup too often. Take my word for it: it works. Sometimes I don't "listen" to my own recipe—instead of serving the soup hot, I serve it chilled the day after I make it. When I'm feeling especially fancy, I top it with crab meat as well as the mascarpone. A knockout!

Serves 4

10 MINUTES PREP TIME
20 MINUTES COOKING TIME

2 tablespoons olive oil

2 tablespoons butter

3 cups green peas, thawed if frozen, ¼ cup reserved for garnish

2 shallots, finely chopped

3 cups vegetable stock

2 tablespoons cream cheese

2 tablespoons heavy cream

¼ cup mascarpone cheese

Zest of 1 lemon

¼ cup chopped Italian parsley

¼ cup chopped mint

Salt and pepper

1. Preheat an oven to 400°F.

2. Place olive oil, butter, peas and shallots on a sheet tray and roast in oven for 8 minutes. While in the oven, heat vegetable stock in a pot until right before boiling. Season stock with salt and pepper.

3. Mix the cream cheese, heavy cream, and mascarpone in a stand mixer until combined and slightly loose—don't whip it too much. Add lemon zest and mix one more time to combine. Season with salt and set aside.

4. When peas are done, add to stock and bring to a rapid boil. Reduce to simmer, add parsley and mint, and cook for 5 minutes.

5. Using a hand or stand blender, blend the soup until silky smooth. If too thick, add a touch of stock or water.

6. Serve soup with a drizzle of the mascarpone mixture in the middle and the reserved fresh peas to garnish.

Roma Tomato and Basil Soup
with Rosemary Focaccia Croutons

Tomato soup was the very first grownup food my son Gage ate—and guess what? He loved it. Ashley and I began feeding him "real" food when most babies were eating nothing but baby food. This soup can be made with fresh tomatoes, canned tomatoes, and even green tomatoes. As a boy, I roamed through the tomato fields looking for green tomato windfall. We'd fry them with a crunchy coating and also make a green tomato soup. I wish I had a fantastic story about tomato soup, but the most I can say about this rendition is that it's a very good example of tomato soup. Homemade soup is a treat, yet a lot of people don't think of making tomato soup, even though it's a great way to salvage tomatoes that are a little past their prime or to use those you grow in the garden—and everyone will love it.

Serves 4 to 6

10 MINUTES PREP TIME
25 MINUTES COOKING TIME

½ cup diced onion

3 pounds ripe Roma tomatoes, diced and excess water removed

3 tablespoons tomato paste

2 tablespoons brown sugar

3 tablespoons white balsamic vinegar

2 cups vegetable stock

½ cup chopped basil

2 cups rosemary and sage croutons, *see recipe p. 251*

Grana Padano cheese, grated, for garnish

Olive oil

Salt and pepper

1. In a large pot on high heat with a drizzle of olive oil, add the onions and cook for 3 minutes. Season with salt and pepper. Add tomatoes and cook for another 5 minutes with the lid on.

2. Add tomato paste and cook for 2 minutes, to allow time for the paste to be incorporated into the mix. Add brown sugar, white balsamic vinegar, and vegetable stock and bring to a boil.

3. Reduce slightly, about 2 minutes, and cook for 13–15 minutes on medium high.

4. Stir basil into the soup. Blend together with an immersion blender to the smoothness that you desire and adjust seasoning. Serve with rosemary and sage croutons and Grana Padano cheese on top.

Roasted Broccoli Soup with Crispy Pancetta and Grana Padano

I don't think I would have created a broccoli soup ten or fifteen years ago, at least not one that I'd encourage you to make all year long. It's true you can get fresh broccoli pretty much year 'round, but it's not always great. (It's kind of sad in February and March.) But luckily frozen broccoli—and lots of other vegetables—is great. For this soup, I roast the broccoli, which may surprise you, but it makes it easier than ever and also brings out the broccoli's hearty, earthy flavor.

Serves 4

10 MINUTES PREP TIME
25 MINUTES COOKING TIME

1 cup diced onion

2 pounds broccoli, chopped into medium pieces

4 cloves peeled garlic

5 stems thyme

½ pound pancetta, diced small

½ teaspoon red chili flakes

4 tablespoons butter

3 quarts vegetable stock

½ cup grated Grana Padano cheese

Salt and pepper

Olive oil

1. Preheat the oven to 425°F.

2. In a large bowl, toss together the onion, broccoli, garlic, thyme and a good drizzle of olive oil. Season with salt and pepper. Place on a sheet tray and cook for 10–12 minutes.

3. While the vegetables are roasting, render the pancetta until crispy in a large stockpot on medium high heat. Place the pancetta on a paper-lined plate and set aside half the fat in a sealable jar to use another time. Then place the red chili flakes, butter and vegetable stock in the pot and bring to a boil.

4. When the vegetables are finished roasting, reserve a few pieces of broccoli for garnish, and add the rest of the vegetables to the boiling stockpot. Cook for another 2 minutes, then transfer into a blender to pulse until very smooth. If too thick, add a touch of water. Adjust seasoning with salt and pepper.

5. Pour soup into bowls and garnish with pancetta, the reserved broccoli and Grana Padano.

FABIO SAYS

Modern technology and attention to quality have made the **frozen vegetable** aisle of the supermarket one of the best places to shop. I always keep frozen vegetables on hand, partly to save on chopping and partly because the broccoli, cauliflower, beans and so on are flash-frozen at their peak and taste great. I still buy loads of fresh vegetables, both at the supermarket and the farmer's market, but if I can't find what I want, I know I can rely on frozen vegetables. I rarely buy spinach frozen, though, because it's so easy to cook fresh and you don't have to worry about squeezing the moisture from a slippery frozen block as it thaws.

Stewed Cauliflower Soup
with Turmeric and Pepperoncini

Honestly, I don't have much to say about this soup except this: it's just a cauliflower soup. I add potatoes for texture and heavy cream for smooth luxuriousness. The soup is topped with pepperoncini for bright flavor, and the turmeric provides vibrant color. Buy cauliflower when it's in season—in the late summer through the fall—and cook it until it's tender.

Serves 4

10 MINUTES PREP TIME
20 MINUTES COOKING TIME

4 tablespoons butter

1 cup diced yellow onion

5 garlic cloves, roughly chopped

1 large head cauliflower, chopped into small pieces

1 cup diced russet potatoes

1 cup half-and-half

1 cup heavy cream

1 cup vegetable stock

½ cup thinly sliced pepperoncini

½ cup extra virgin olive oil

1 teaspoon turmeric

Salt and pepper

1. Place the butter in a large pot on medium high heat to melt. Add the yellow onion and garlic to cook for 3–5 minutes, then add the cauliflower and potatoes to cook for another 4 minutes.

2. Add the half-and-half, heavy cream and vegetable stock and bring just to a boil. Cook for 10 to 12 minutes at this heat, then adjust seasoning. Transfer to a high powered blender and then, in batches, blend until very smooth. If it's too thick for your liking, add a touch of water.

3. Once soup is finished, garnish with pepperoncinis. Mix the extra virgin olive oil with turmeric and drizzle on top for a bright, vibrant finish. Add salt and pepper to taste.

Asparagus Soup with Basil Pesto and Tarragon Grape Salad

Italians love asparagus and cook it in a variety of ways. I'm not as crazy about it as some people are (the reason for this, I suspect, is because it makes your pee smell bad and I don't like that!), but along with my compatriots, I recognize its culinary potential.

For this soup I boil the asparagus in broth and wine, but when I have big fat stalks I prefer roasting them. Very skinny stalks taste like charred matchsticks when they're roasted and do better steamed or even left raw. When I have a lot of fat asparagus, I shave the stalks and toss the shavings in raw salads.

You'll discover with this recipe that pesto and asparagus do well together; the pesto brightens the overall flavor of the soup. And the grape salad garnish is fun and pretty.

Serves 4

10 TO 15 MINUTES PREP TIME
20 MINUTES COOKING TIME

¼ cup white wine

4 cups vegetable broth

2 bay leaves

2 pounds fresh asparagus, chopped coarsely (and a few thin slices for garnish)

2 teaspoons fresh thyme

2 tablespoons butter

½ cup half-and-half

1 teaspoon minced fresh tarragon

½ cup halved red grapes

12 leaves whole tarragon, for garnish

½ cup basil pesto, store-bought or homemade

Salt and pepper

Olive oil

1. Combine the white wine, broth, bay leaves, asparagus and thyme in a large pot and bring to a boil. Cook for 5 minutes until asparagus has softened. Add the butter and half-and-half and cook for another minute. Season with salt and pepper.

2. Remove bay leaves and blend until smooth with immersion blender.

3. In a small bowl, toss the thin slices of asparagus together with the minced tarragon, grapes and whole tarragon and a touch of olive oil, salt and pepper.

4. Garnish soup with pesto and top with grape salad.

FABIO SAYS

They say **asparagus** can teach you something about yourself. If you boil asparagus, it turns soft and mushy. If you boil an egg, it hardens. What does this mean? That life's circumstances show you what you are and what you're made of.

Braised Carrot Soup
with Farro and Parsley Salad

In Italy, carrots are never fancy. They're sold in big bunches and are so inexpensive people buy more than they need. Once home, the carrots aren't refrigerated but are left in the pantry. This is how you should store carrots; they go bad faster in the refrigerator. On the other hand, the bunch of carrots left in the pantry often are forgotten and start to wilt. So pathetic and sad! At this point they are a step away from the trash can, yet there's a silver lining because their carrot flavor is so concentrated that the vegetables make fantastic soup.

If you have big, old carrots and want to make this soup, you could roast them instead of braising. Roast them in a 350º to 375ºF oven for 10 to 25 minutes (the time depends on the size of the carrots) until you can run through them with a fork.

Serves 4

15 MINUTES PREP TIME
30 MINUTES COOKING TIME

1 ¼ quarts chicken stock

1 pound carrots, peeled and chopped coarsely

½ cup uncooked farro, or barley if not available

2 tablespoons butter

1 onion, minced

3 cloves garlic, minced

2 teaspoons dried thyme

¾ cup whole milk

¼ cup orange juice

1 teaspoon rice wine vinegar

1 tablespoon minced fresh chives

¼ cup carrots sliced very thin, for garnish (if desired)

¼ cup Italian parsley leaves, torn

Olive oil

Salt and pepper

1. In a pot on high heat, bring the stock and carrots to a boil. Allow to cook until carrots are fully softened and broken down, about 13–15 minutes. While cooking, bring a pot of salted water to a boil, then dump in farro and cook for 10 minutes.

2. While the two pots are cooking, grab a large sauté pan and place on medium high heat. Melt the butter, then add the onion and cook for 3 minutes. Season with salt and pepper, then add the garlic and cook for another minute. Add the dried thyme, whole milk and orange juice, bring to a boil, and then turn off.

3. Once this mixture is done and the carrots are cooked, add both mixtures into a blender and blend until very smooth. Adjust seasoning with salt and pepper. By this time the farro should be cooked. Drain and cool at room temperature.

4. In a small bowl, toss together the vinegar, chives, sliced carrots and parsley. Add a drizzle of olive oil and season to taste with salt and pepper. Ladle soup into bowls and garnish with the cooled farro and the parsley salad.

FABIO SAYS

Have you ever wondered what to do with the **wine** at the bottom of the bottle at the end of the evening? Freeze it in ice cube trays to use later in soups and sauces. You'll only need one or two cubes to flavor, add to a pan sauce, or drop in a beef stew to melt into the other flavors.

Cream of Potato Soup with Rosemary and Caramelized Shallots

As with carrots, Italians can't buy a few potatoes. We buy them in five-, ten-, or twenty-pound bags and, just like carrots, we store them in the pantry—never in the refrigerator. Although soup is not a fundamental part of an Italian meal, we tend to make it in the wintertime when we work long hours and it gets dark early. Minestrone is a popular soup, but so is a creamy potato like this one, garnished with shallots and rosemary. Beyond soup, we mash, broil and fry potatoes—when she has a big bag, my mom cooks them all week long.

Serves 4

10 MINUTES PREP TIME
25 MINUTES COOKING TIME

½ cup olive oil, divided in half

10 cloves garlic

10 shallots, peeled and sliced

½ cup dry white wine

2 teaspoons chopped fresh thyme

4 sprigs rosemary, pulled from stem and divided in half

3 cups medium russet potatoes, diced

1 ½ quarts chicken stock

½ cup heavy cream

½ cup whole milk

Extra virgin olive oil

Salt and pepper

1. In a large pot on medium high heat, drizzle in ¼ cup olive oil, then add the garlic. Cook the garlic until it starts to brown, about 3–4 minutes. Add shallots and cook for 7 minutes to caramelize. Season with salt and pepper, then reserve some of the shallots to use as garnish when the soup is finished.

2. Deglaze pot with white wine and bring to a boil. Reduce wine on high heat for 2 minutes. Add the thyme, half of the rosemary, potatoes and chicken stock. Bring back to a boil and cook for 10 minutes, then reduce heat to medium and cook for another 5 minutes. Adjust seasoning with salt and pepper.

3. Add the cream and milk and heat through. Place all contents in a blender and blend until very smooth. If too thick for your liking, adjust consistency with water, a touch at a time.

4. Place remaining ¼ cup olive oil in a small sauté pan on medium heat and wait until hot. Add remaining rosemary and flash fry for 10–15 seconds until bright green. Scoop out with slotted spoon and dry with paper towels on a plate.

5. To serve, ladle soup into bowls and garnish with set-aside shallots, fried rosemary, and a drizzle of extra virgin olive oil.

FABIO SAYS

If your potatoes sprout green buds, put an apple in the plastic bag with them. This will slow down the buds' development.

Cremini and Shiitake Roasted Mushroom Bisque with Rosemary "Chips"

Serves 4

15 MINUTES PREP TIME
20 MINUTES COOKING TIME

1 pound cremini mushrooms,
sliced

1 pound shiitake mushrooms,
sliced and stems removed

2 tablespoons dried thyme

¼ cup minced celery

½ cup minced onion

1 cup heavy cream

2 cups chicken stock

2 tablespoons chopped
fresh rosemary

½ cup grated Grana Padano

Salt and pepper

Olive oil

1. Heat a large Dutch oven to a high heat and drizzle in a good amount of olive oil. Add the mushrooms and cook until caramelized, about 8–10 minutes. Season with salt and pepper, add the thyme, celery and onion, and cook for another 3 minutes.

2. Add heavy cream and chicken stock and bring to a boil. Reduce to a simmer and cook for another 5 minutes. Adjust seasoning with salt and pepper.

3. Ladle into a blender and blend until super smooth. Keep warm back in the pot.

4. Mix together rosemary and cheese. Using a tablespoon measurement, spoon two of them in a pile on a plate. Spread out slightly and place in the microwave. Cook for 2 minutes then remove from the plate immediately. Lay on another plate to cool and harden.

5. Ladle soup into shallow bowls and garnish each with rosemary chips.

FABIO SAYS

The **mushroom soups** here and on page 69 are a little nutty and warming and just right for chilly autumn nights and the long, dark winter. For the bisque, the mushrooms are roasted until they're caramelized and their flavor is bursting from them. For the braised soup, the shiitake mushrooms are braised and then mixed with orzo for a simple, nourishing soup that's a little lighter than the bisque. That first soup is a touch more complex, relying on two kinds of mushrooms and then heavy cream to smooth it out.

Braised Mushroom and Orzo Soup with Celery Salad and Grana Padano

Serves 4 to 6

12 MINUTES PREP TIME

30 MINUTES COOKING TIME

2 tablespoons butter

2 tablespoons olive oil

½ cup thinly sliced celery, some reserved for garnish

1 cup peeled and diced carrots

1 cup sliced onions

1 cup thinly sliced fennel, some reserved for garnish

2 teaspoons fresh thyme leaves

1 pound cleaned and sliced shiitake mushrooms

1 pound sliced fresh white mushrooms

4 cups chicken stock

2 cups beef stock

⅔ cup uncooked orzo

½ cup grated Grana Padano cheese, for garnish

Salt and pepper

1. Melt the butter and oil in a stockpot over high heat. Add the celery, carrots, onions and fennel. Cook and stir until tender, about 6 to 7 minutes. Season with salt and pepper.

2. Stir in the thyme and mushrooms and continue cooking until mushrooms are soft, about 6 minutes.

3. Pour chicken and beef stock into the pot, and adjust seasoning with salt and pepper. Cover, bring to a boil, add orzo, and lower to simmer for 15 minutes. Ladle into bowls, and serve with cheese and reserved thinly sliced vegetables sprinkled on the top.

Baby Spinach and Mozzarella Tortellini "in Brodo"

What do Italian mothers give their kids when they're sick? The best chicken soup, of course. When you're feeling a little better, she drops some cheese-filled tortellini in the *brodo* (or broth). Use a good brand of store-bought tortellini rather than going to the trouble of making your own (although you could). The shape is tricky to get right. Or you could make ravioli instead, which is a lot easier (see the recipe on page 97). I'm not ashamed to suggest store-bought tortellini because . . . why not?

Serves 4 to 6

10 MINUTES PREP TIME
20 MINUTES COOKING TIME

2 tablespoons olive oil

5 tablespoons butter

3 bay leaves

4 sprigs fresh thyme

3 quarts chicken broth

1 pound store-bought cheese tortellini, thawed

4 cups baby spinach

¼ cup grated Grana Padano cheese

Extra virgin olive oil, for garnish

Salt and pepper

1. In a large pot on high heat, add the olive oil, butter, bay leaves, thyme and chicken broth. Bring to a boil, and cook for another 7 minutes. Strain, then place back into the pot and return to a boil. Add the tortellini and cook in the stock for 5 minutes.

2. Remove from heat, add spinach, and let it cook off heat for 3 minutes. Adjust seasoning with salt and pepper, drizzle with extra virgin olive oil, and serve in bowls with grated cheese on top.

Braised Pork, Sweet Date and Kale Stew

Don't be afraid to cook with dates. These sweet fruits are perfect with pork and turn this ordinary stew into something extraordinary.

Serves 4–6

15 MINUTES PREP TIME

30 MINUTES COOKING TIME

2 tablespoons
extra-virgin olive oil

8 ounces pork belly,
cut into ½-inch chunks

1 large leek, white and pale
green parts only, diced small

1 large onion, diced small

2 bay leaves

2 carrots, diced small

2 stalks celery, diced small

3 medium cloves garlic,
sliced thin

3 stems rosemary

10 dates, sliced

10 stems thyme

1 bunch kale, stems removed,
leaves roughly chopped

2 quarts homemade or
store-bought chicken stock

1 cup beef demi-glace

⅓ cup white balsamic
vinegar

Salt and pepper

1. Heat olive oil in a large Dutch oven over medium heat. Add pork belly and cook until lightly browned, about 7 minutes.

2. Add the leek, onion, bay leaves, carrot, celery, garlic, rosemary, dates and thyme. Season with salt and pepper and cook, scraping up browned bits from the bottom, about 10 minutes.

3. Add in the kale, stock, and demi-glace. Season with salt and pepper, cover and bring to a boil. Reduce to a simmer and add vinegar. Cook for another 13–15 minutes, until vegetables are soft and pork is tender.

PASTA

As far as I'm concerned, the world has Italy to thank for three things: the beauty of the country itself, the Renaissance, and pasta.

Everything I am I owe to pasta. It made me what I am. I grew up eating pasta, learned how to make it at a very early age, and have never stopped either eating it or making it. When I was a boy, my mom might ask me if I was hungry after school. Eager to get outside and away from the school books, I told her no! I ate at school. If she said okay but I'm cooking pasta, I'd usually relent and stay home for a little while. My mom's pasta is hard to resist!

Pasta is made from flour and water or flour and eggs. Nothing else. About as basic as you can get, which may be why in Italy we eat it for lunch and dinner, day after day. Many Italians still make their own—I do—which is another reason why the best Italian food is found in private homes, not restaurants. Pasta made with durum wheat flour and water is usually cut into ribbons or strands, like spaghetti or fettuccine, and used for light, quick dishes. This is the pasta that holds its "al dente" texture the best.

Pasta made from flour and eggs is a little fuller and more substantial than pasta made from just flour and water, as you'll see once you read through the recipes on the following pages. While egg pasta can very successfully be cut into ribbons, it's also the dough you want when you have a longer game plan and will maybe make ravioli or tortellini. It's easy to make, especially if you use the food processor, as I do.

No one wants to eat overcooked pasta, which stays in your stomach like a rock. Not good. If you cook pasta from a box, follow the instructions on the package, but cook it for less than the recommended time—sometimes as much as 60 percent of the suggested time. Al dente pasta tastes better and encourages more chewing. More chewing, better digestion. More pasta, better life.

FABIO SAYS

With so much good to very good pasta for sale, why make your own? I say, why not? It's a labor of love that used to make a mess and take some time as you piled the flour on the counter, dug a well in the center, and cracked eggs into it before working it into a dough. But no more! I've created a version that takes three minutes and because it's all done in the food processor, there's no mess. And it's perfect, just like Grandma used to make.

There's nothing exotic about handmade pasta in the present-day Viviani household. Here's why. When I was a little kid, we lived with my grandparents and great-grandmother, and it was my great-grandma who took on the job of "babysitting" the rambunctious young Fabio. One way she kept me occupied and blessedly quiet was to hand me half a dozen or more eggs, flour and a large board. I would spend hours cracking eggs, working them into the flour, and then making pasta, which explains why today, making pasta is second nature to me. Soon, she and I were cooking entire meals together and I became (somewhat annoyingly, I am sure) proprietary about these meals, even bragging to my first-grade teacher that I didn't really need school because I could already cook dinner. And so a chef was "born."

When you make pasta, the goal is to create a dough that can be dried once it's rolled and cut into strands, or shaped into short shapes with a pasta maker that attaches to a standing mixer. I cut pasta strands like fettuccine and then twist them into lose nests to dry on a tray. Once dry, I can store them in a large, gallon-size plastic tub with a tight-fitting lid (I expel as much air as I can) for two or three weeks. In our household, that translates to ten or fifteen portions ready to be dropped in boiling, salted water when it's time for dinner.

When I make stubbier pasta, I generally start with three to four pounds of pasta, shape it, and freeze it in eight- to ten-ounce freezer bags. Those will keep for five to six months. A word of warning: don't freeze the pasta without shaping it—if you do, you'll have a lump of frozen dough that will never defrost to the right consistency for shaping. Once it defrosts, the composition of the ingredients changes. On the other hand, shaped pasta pieces that have been frozen can go directly into boiling, salted water, no defrosting necessary.

When you make this dough, don't try to double or triple the recipe; it won't fit in the food processor. (But it's so easy, you can make it a few times over.) If it's too wet and gooey, add a little flour. If it's too dry, add an egg yolk. The formula I developed should work perfectly, but factors such as the humidity of the day and the size of the eggs can make a difference.

The first recipe here is for traditional pasta, made with refined white flour. The next is for whole-wheat pasta. A lot of people prefer the latter for its health benefits—more fiber, protein, and other nutrients—and mild nuttiness. Because whole wheat pasta is not as elastic as traditional, it's also going to be more al dente, have more bite, when it's cooked.

Finally, I have a recipe for gluten-free pasta. It won't taste exactly like fresh pasta, but it is as close as you can get. It's a lot nicer than the pre-made gluten-free varieties on the market and won't taste like cardboard. The ingredients are a little hard to find, but certainly not impossible!

Fresh Egg Pasta

Serves 3 to 4

10 MINUTES PREP TIME

2 egg yolks

4 whole eggs

Pinch of salt

½ teaspoon pepper

1 teaspoon olive oil

2 cups flour,
plus extra on the side
(in case eggs are
bigger than usual)

1. Place the egg yolks and whole eggs in a food processor using the blade attachment. Add the salt, pepper and olive oil, and pulse a few times.

2. Add half of the flour and pulse until the eggs absorb it and you have a semi-thick paste. Add the rest of the flour and allow the blade to rotate continuously. When the dough is ready, you should see a ball-shaped mass of dough bouncing around the canister. If the dough is still too wet to the touch, add an extra tablespoon of flour. If it is a bit dry, add a little water.

3. Take the pasta dough out and roll/shape according to the directions of the recipe you are making. If you're saving some of the unshaped dough for later, wrap it in plastic wrap and place it in the fridge for up to six days.

FABIO SAYS

If you've ever wondered if the **eggs** stowed at the back of your refrigerator are fresh, here's a test that will help. Fill a bowl with about 4 inches of water and dunk the eggs. If they stay on the bottom of the bowl, they are fresh. If they tip upright, they are pretty fresh. If they float to the surface, they're well past their prime.

Whole Wheat Pasta

Serves 3 to 4

10 MINUTES PREP TIME

1 teaspoon salt

1 cup all-purpose flour

1 ¼ cups whole wheat
pastry flour

4 whole eggs

2 egg yolks

3 tablespoons water

1 tablespoon olive oil

Flour for dusting

1. Place salt, all-purpose flour and whole wheat flour in a food processor and pulse to combine. Set the food processor on constant and add 1 egg at a time, finishing with the yolks. Add the water in 1 tablespoon at a time, and finish by adding the olive oil. Make sure to check the consistency of the dough—as soon as the dough begins to come together, take it out.

2. On a dusted work surface, knead dough for about 2 minutes. It should feel pliable and easy to stretch. If the dough is too wet, add more flour a little bit at a time until it feels slightly harder than Play-Doh. It should be very smooth.

3. Let the dough rest wrapped in plastic for 20–30 minutes. At this stage you can follow whatever recipe you have based on the shapes you want to eat. We recommend using the orecchiette shape for this dough. Since the dough is slightly heartier, it is very easy to mold and it holds its shape when cooked.

FABIO SAYS

I always cook **pasta** in salted water and urge you to do the same. And I always use a lot of water for the pasta; you should, too—at least five to six quarts of water for one pound of pasta. If you wonder how much salt to add to the water once it comes to a boil, think "handful." If you've an oversized hand, make it half a handful; if you've a very small hand, make it two handfuls. You get the idea. Be generous, not ridiculous, with the salt. It makes the pasta taste better.

Gluten-Free Pasta

Serves 2 to 3

20 MINUTES PREP TIME
5 MINUTES COOKING TIME

1 teaspoon fine sea salt
1 teaspoon guar gum
2 teaspoons xanthan gum
½ cup potato starch
½ cup quinoa flour
⅔ cup corn flour
2 eggs
4 egg yolks

1. Sift sea salt, guar gum, xanthan gum, potato starch, quinoa flour and corn flour together twice. Place into a stand mixer. Make a bowl of the dry ingredients, and put the eggs and egg yolks into the center. Run the stand mixer with paddle attachment on medium speed about 3 minutes. The final dough should feel firm yet still pliable.

2. Shape the pasta into small cylinders by rubbing it with the palms of your hands. This shape works well with the delicate texture of the dough.

3. Bring a pot of salted water to a boil. Cook pasta for 3–5 minutes. Taste the pasta as it cooks and remove when it reaches the texture you enjoy most.

FABIO SAYS

As much as I hope you'll make your own pasta, I know that most people buy **pasta in a box**. My best advice is to stick with known brands in the supermarket, not because I endorse any of them, but because these companies have a long tradition of making boxed pasta and can tell you how to cook it with instructions on the side of the box. Of course, I don't think you should follow them; instead cut the recommended cooking time by a few minutes so you get al dente pasta. I've been known to cut it to 60 percent of the suggested time for al dente. Use your best judgment. You can also be more adventuresome and buy fresh pasta from your local gourmet shop. It won't be as dry as the boxed pasta and will take less time to cook.

The best advice I can give you is to make sure the pasta you buy is the right shape for the sauce. Chunky sauces need something like penne with ridges and a hollowed center to catch the ingredients. Other shapes work well for this kind of sauce, too, like twisted fusilli and farfalle, or bow ties. Thinner, smoother sauces work best with strands of pasta, like spaghetti or linguine.

That said, I hope you'll make your own pasta. You can thank me later!

Classic Fusilli with Sausage and Peppers

When you choose the pasta to go with a sauce as rich and chunky as this, choose fusilli. Its corkscrew shape is the perfect one to catch the sausage and peppers mixed with the rich, easy sauce. I also like to team fusilli with a coarse homemade pesto. The basil and pine nuts cling to the pasta's nooks and crannies.

Serves 4 to 6

15 MINUTES PREP TIME
20 MINUTES COOKING TIME

½ pound sweet Italian sausage, ground

2 tablespoons minced garlic

½ cup diced onion

¼ cup sliced yellow bell pepper

½ cup sliced red bell pepper

1 cup sliced orange bell pepper

1 pound dried fusilli pasta

1 cup white wine

1 cup chicken stock

2 tablespoons extra-virgin olive oil

¼ cup chopped Italian parsley

1 stick of butter

Grana Padano cheese, grated, for garnish

Salt and pepper

Olive oil

1. Bring a pot of salted water to a boil.

2. In a second large pot on high heat, add a drizzle of olive oil then put in sausage. Cook for 3 minutes then add garlic and onions. Season with salt and pepper. Cook for another minute.

3. Add yellow, red, and orange peppers and cook mixture for 5 minutes. Adjust seasoning.

4. Add pasta to water and cook for 6 minutes.

5. Deglaze pot with white wine and reduce sauce by half on high heat. Add chicken stock and reduce by half again. When stock is reduced, add pasta, extra-virgin olive oil, parsley, and butter. Stir until butter is melted and has formed a sauce with pasta and stock. Garnish with Grana Padano to finish.

Potato and Cheese Gnocchi Dough

Making gnocchi is similar to making pasta, although you need a potato to round out the dough. I suggest using a baked potato, because boiled potatoes are too moist for the dough. Bake the potato for about an hour and fifteen minutes, let it cool, then peel it and mash it roughly before putting it in the standing mixer fitted with the paddle attachment. The mixer makes this dough super easy and reduces mess. I don't like mess when I cook; I don't have a housemaid to clean up after me, so I like to use the mixer. You will, too. This recipe does not come with a sauce because once you perfect the dough, just about anything goes—olive oil and cheese, tomato sauce. It's all okay.

Serves 4

10 MINUTES PREP TIME
30 MINUTES COOKING TIME

1 teaspoon pepper

1 teaspoon grated nutmeg

2 teaspoons salt

½ cup flour,
plus more set aside

½ cup grated
Grana Padano cheese

2 ½ pounds baked Idaho
potato, skin removed, cooled

1. In a stand mixer with the paddle attachment, mix pepper, nutmeg, salt, flour and Grana Padano together and let blend for 2 minutes.

2. Add the potato and let mix on medium low speed for 5–6 minutes. Feel the dough. If still sticky, add a touch more flour. You should have smooth, soft dough.

3. Flour a surface and cut dough into chunks to roll into dough snakes. Cut snakes into bite-size pieces.

4. Place gnocchi in a pot of boiling salted water, not crowding each other. When the first 4 or 5 start to float, remove and toss with preferred sauce.

Red Wine Spaghetti
with Belgian Endive and Gorgonzola

I love all pasta but spaghetti is my go-to, every time, hands down. Italy is a country of spaghetti lovers, and we eat more spaghetti than anyone.

This spaghetti gets its hue from the red wine added to the cooking water, a technique that is more for visual impact than flavor. Use any wine you have around or mix several together if you have partially filled bottles left over from earlier meals. This is one time you don't need to break out the good stuff; use less expensive vino for the pasta. The red pasta is offset by the bright white endive, a bitter lettuce whose flavor is smoothed out by the shallots and garlic.

Serves 3 to 4

10 MINUTES PREP TIME
15 MINUTES COOKING TIME

1 bottle red wine,
such as a Pinot Noir

½ pound dried spaghetti

¼ cup extra-virgin olive oil

1 large shallot, halved,
thinly sliced into strips

3 large cloves garlic, chopped

2 Belgian endives,
cut into thin strips

¼ cup white wine

½ cup vegetable stock

6 tablespoons butter

½ cup gorgonzola cheese

Salt and pepper

1. In a pot of salted water, about 2 quarts, pour in bottle of red wine. Bring to a boil and drop in spaghetti.

2. While pasta cooks, heat a large pan with olive oil on medium high heat. Add the shallots and garlic, and cook for 3 minutes to soften. Then add endive and cook for another 3 to 4 minutes. Season with salt and pepper.

3. Deglaze with white wine and vegetable stock. Reduce by half, then swirl in butter until it melts and forms a sauce.

4. After spaghetti has cooked to preferred doneness, drain and add pasta to the sauce pan. Toss together until sauce coats pasta and crumble cheese on top.

Poor Man's Carbonara: Linguine with Crispy Guanciale and Creamy Poached Egg

Italians don't agree on much, but we all agree on how to make a good carbonara—and that we love football (soccer). If the omelet is the measure by which French chefs are judged, then carbonaras are the measure for Italian home cooks. If your mom can't make a good carbonara, then she can't cook! Sorry about that. This is the quintessential dish for people who enjoy food and life—creamy, cheesy, and so easy. And I make it with crispy guanciale—an Italian cured pork that's heavy on the fat—rather than the more traditional bacon.

Serves 4

10 MINUTES PREP TIME
20 MINUTES COOKING TIME

1 pound dried linguine
1 tablespoon vinegar
2 tablespoons butter
1 cup diced guanciale*
2 garlic cloves, chopped
2 shallots, sliced thin
1 cup chicken stock
4 eggs
½ cup heavy cream
½ cup grated
Grana Padano cheese
Salt and pepper

1. Bring a pot of salted water to a boil and drop in pasta. Cook the pasta about 7–9 minutes, while bringing a small pot of water with 1 tablespoon of vinegar to a simmer for the eggs.

2. Meanwhile, heat the butter in a large pot on medium heat and add the guanciale. Render it until just crispy, about 7–8 minutes. Add the garlic and shallots and cook for another 2 minutes.

3. Add the chicken stock, bring to a boil, and reduce by half. Season with salt and pepper.

4. Swirl the vinegar water with a spoon or whisk. As you're doing this, crack each egg and carefully drop it into the swirling water so that the whites wrap around the yolks. Cook for 4 minutes. Carefully remove and place on a plate that has been wrapped tightly with plastic wrap.

5. Add cream to the pasta sauce and reduce by half. Once reduced, add pasta to sauce. Toss the pasta, then incorporate the cheese. The pasta should be very creamy, but not too thick. Place in bowls and serve with an egg on top of each.

*If guanciale isn't available, use pancetta.

Cavatappi with "Italian Chorizo" and Braised Beans

The sauce for this cooks as quickly as the pasta, and while I love to make my own pasta, boxed cavatappi is just fine. What you need is chunky macaroni. You could use black or pinto beans instead of white beans, and naturally, canned are just fine. I am calling spicy Italian sausage "Italian chorizo," but if you have the "real thing"—i.e., chorizo—feel free to use it.

Serves 3 to 4

10 MINUTES PREP TIME
20 MINUTES COOKING TIME

2 tablespoons vegetable oil

1 teaspoon red chili flakes

¾ cup minced onion

8 ounces spicy Italian sausage, cooked and sliced into ¼-inch-thick rounds

1 cup canned great northern beans, rinsed

2 cups chicken broth

8 ounces dried cavatappi pasta

5 tablespoons butter

½ cup arugula

½ cup Grana Padano cheese

Salt and pepper

1. Bring a large pot of salted water to a boil. While water is starting to boil, add oil to a skillet. Add the red chili flakes, onion and sausage and cook for 5 minutes on medium high heat. Season with salt and pepper.

2. Stir in the beans and broth. Bring to a boil and reduce by half, about 6–7 minutes.

3. When water is boiling, add cavatappi and cook until desired doneness, around 5–6 minutes for al dente.

4. Once broth mixture is reduced, turn heat to low and melt in butter to form the sauce. Add the arugula and cooked pasta. Stir pasta until sauce coats it. Adjust seasoning with salt and pepper. If sauce has reduced too much, add a touch of pasta water.

5. Mix half the cheese into the pasta, then when plating, use the other half as garnish.

Fettuccine with Salmon, Dill and Zucchini Ribbons

This is a great looking-dish, and if you're like me and like salmon with dill and tarragon, you'll be in heaven with this one. As the salmon cooks, it breaks down a little and yields a nice sauce. Top it with zucchini ribbons, and you have yourself a winner. I use one of those veggie spaghetti makers for the ribbons but you can just as easily use a mandoline or vegetable peeler.

Serves 3 to 4

10 MINUTES PREP TIME
20 MINUTES COOKING TIME

2 shallots, sliced thin

1 small zucchini, shaved into ribbons

8 ounces cubed salmon, skin removed

1 pound fresh fettuccine, *see recipe for fresh pasta, p. 80*

1 tablespoon chopped tarragon

2 tablespoons chopped dill

2 tablespoons chopped parsley

4 tablespoons extra virgin olive oil

8 tablespoons butter

⅓ cup grated Grana Padano cheese

Salt and pepper

Olive oil

1. Bring a pot of salted water to a boil.

2. Heat a large pan on medium high and add a drizzle of olive oil. Add the shallots and cook for 4 minutes. Add the zucchini ribbons, season with salt and pepper, and cook for another minute.

3. Add the salmon to the pan and drop the pasta in the water at the same time. Cook the salmon for just 2–3 minutes, as not to overcook it. Add the tarragon, dill, parsley, extra virgin olive oil and butter. Once butter melts, add a touch of the pasta water to create an emulsified sauce.

4. Add the pasta to the sauce, fold in the Grana Padano, and toss. Adjust seasoning and add pasta water as needed to keep consistency.

Fresh Ravioli with Ricotta and Roasted Spinach in Light Olive Oil and Tomato Sauce

All you need for ravioli is fresh pasta dough and you're halfway there—remember to shape the dough as soon as you make it (see the recipe on page 80). Use a cookie cutter to cut out two-inch squares or circles for filling (rectangles are awkward to fill and fold so skip 'em). The spinach is roasted, so it's not damp and needs no squeezing. As it roasts, it kind of wilts and browns on the edges, at which time it becomes easy to chop in the food processor or with a knife and then mix with the cheese. I like to make three or four dozen raviolis to keep in the freezer and then, when we're hungry, just pop them in boiling, salted water until cooked through, which takes minutes. These cheese and spinach ravioli are served with a simple tomato sauce. So easy and satisfying.

Serves 6 to 8

15 MINUTES PREP TIME
15 MINUTES COOKING TIME

FOR THE PASTA:

1 pound fresh pasta, cut into 2-inch squares, *see recipe for pasta dough, p. 80*

Flour, for dusting

FOR THE FILLING:

3 cups fresh spinach

¼ cup olive oil

1 ¼ cup ricotta cheese

2 eggs, beaten

FOR THE SAUCE:

½ cup olive oil

½ cup torn basil

4 cloves garlic, minced

4 Roma tomatoes, sliced thin

Salt and pepper

Grana Padano cheese, for grating

1. Preheat the oven to 400°F.

2. Bring a large pot of salted water to a boil. Spread the pasta on counter with a touch of flour underneath.

3. Place spinach onto a sheet tray and bake for 10 minutes. Cool slightly.

4. To make the filling: in a large bowl, mix together the spinach, olive oil and ricotta cheese, and season with salt and pepper. *(You can make this mixture a day in advance to help cut prep time.)*

5. With a pastry brush, and working in small batches so that the egg doesn't dry out, lightly brush the pasta squares with beaten eggs. Once all are brushed, spoon 1 tablespoon of filling in the middle of each. Fold into a triangle and push out all the air with your fingers. Run your fingers along the edges ensuring that the ravioli is sealed.

6. To make the sauce: in a large pan on medium high heat, add olive oil, basil, garlic and tomatoes. Cook while stirring for 5–7 minutes. Look for the tomato to break down completely to form a sauce. Adjust seasoning and set aside.

7. Drop the raviolis in the boiling water, 6 at a time. Cook each batch for 2 to 3 minutes, remove from the pot, and place into the sauce with a touch of the pasta water. Repeat. Serve a little sauce with each ravioli. Garnish with grated Grana Padano.

FABIO SAYS

Tomatoes don't belong in the fridge until they are cut. Ditto for citrus fruit. The low temperature degrades the aroma and flavor of these persnickety fruits. Once they are sliced open, they should be stored in the refrigerator inside plastic bags or protected by plastic wrap.

Skillet Orecchiette
with Tarragon and Lump Crab

Lots of flavor going on here. To me, tarragon just makes food more delicious. It's sort of like the result of a marriage between basil and mint, with the tarragon not as subtle as basil and not as cool as mint. Top this pasta with good lump crab, not that cheap imitation in the freezer case. Fresh from the fishmonger is best, but you won't go to jail or hell for using high-quality canned lump crab. The compound butter just adds another layer of flavor.

Serves 4

15 MINUTES PREP TIME
20 MINUTES COOKING TIME

½ pound
dried orecchiette pasta

1 teaspoon minced
fresh thyme

4 tablespoons olive oil

1 shallot, minced

2 garlic cloves, minced

½ cup dry white wine

¼ cup heavy cream

1 ½ cups chicken stock

5 tablespoons dill,
tarragon and lemon butter,
see recipe p. 243

½ pound lump crab meat

Torn tarragon, for garnish

Salt and pepper

1. Heat a pot of salted water to a boil. Add the pasta and cook for 6–7 minutes.

2. While pasta is cooking, put another pot on medium high heat and add the thyme, olive oil, shallot and garlic. Cook for 3 minutes, then deglaze with white wine. Cook for another minute.

3. Add the heavy cream and chicken stock. Reduce sauce by half, around 5 minutes, then add pasta with a touch of cooking water to the pot.

4. Once the sauce is reduced, add tarragon butter and crab meat. Stir into pasta off the heat until very creamy.

Rigatoni with Roasted Shrimp, Marinated Crab and Red Pepper Sauce

This is one of those dishes where the flavors just keep coming, bite after bite. The classic sauce is made with earthy roasted red peppers as well as tomatoes—perfect with the seafood. I like to mix shrimp and crab to bolster the flavor of each and make the dish come together.

Serves 3 to 4

15 MINUTES PREP TIME
20 MINUTES COOKING TIME

1 tablespoon oregano

½ cup seafood stock

1 cup roasted red
bell peppers

1 cup whole peeled canned
tomatoes

2 cloves garlic

2 shallots, roughly chopped

½ pound dried rigatoni pasta

½ pound shrimp, tail-off,
21–25 ct.

½ pound lump crab meat

½ cup torn basil

Extra virgin olive oil

Salt and pepper

1. Place a large pot of salted water on high heat and bring to a boil.

2. While water is starting to boil, place the oregano, seafood stock, red bell peppers, tomatoes, garlic and shallots in a pot and bring right to a boil. Take off the heat and place in a blender. Blend until all ingredients are combined. This will be the sauce.

3. When water is boiling, add the pasta and cook to preferred doneness, about 7 minutes for al dente.

4. Drizzle extra virgin olive oil into another large pot on medium high heat. Add the shrimp and season with salt and pepper. Cook for 2 minutes, then add the crab. Cook for another minute, then add basil and finish with the pepper sauce. Turn the heat to low.

5. Once pasta is cooked, add to the sauce pot and incorporate. Adjust seasoning with salt and pepper and drizzle with additional extra virgin olive oil to finish.

Linguine with White Wine Lime Butter and Jumbo Lump Crab

A classic, refined linguine dish made with elegant lump crab in place of the more expected clams. And as a zingy topper, I stir a good amount of the lime zest into the sauce. Wow!

Serves 4 to 6

12 MINUTES PREP TIME
30 MINUTES COOKING TIME

½ pound dried linguine pasta
½ cup minced onion
8 garlic cloves, minced
½ cup dry white wine
¾ cup chicken stock
Juice of 4 limes
8 tablespoons butter
¼ cup minced fresh parsley
1 pound jumbo lump crab
Salt and pepper
Olive oil
Lime zest, to garnish

1. Bring a pot of salted water to a boil. Drop in linguine.

2. In a large pot on high heat, add a good drizzle of olive oil. Add the onions and garlic, then cook for 3 minutes. Season with salt and pepper.

3. Deglaze with white wine and reduce by half. Add chicken stock and lime juice and reduce again by half.

4. After cooking pasta for about 8 minutes, add it to the other pot to finish cooking to form the sauce. Add butter and parsley and cook until sauce is thickened, about 3–4 minutes. Reduce heat once sauce starts to form.

5. Fold in lump crab and garnish with fresh lime zest.

Fusilli Pasta with Roasted Garlic, Clams and Cockles Arrabbiata

Arrabbiata means "angry" in Italian, and here it refers to the spiciness of the tomato sauce. The corkscrew pasta fusilli is perfect for catching bits and pieces of this chunky sauce made with little clams and cockles. I like to use two different kinds of clams in seafood sauces; in this recipe use your favorite clams and some cockles. When you do, go easy with the salt, both in the pasta water and when seasoning the sauce. The clams provide a good amount.

Serves 4

10 MINUTES PREP TIME
15 TO 20 MINUTES COOKING TIME

1 pound fusilli pasta

1 teaspoon red chili flakes

¼ cup chopped Fresno chili

¼ cup olive oil

6 cloves garlic, minced

16 clams, cleaned

16 cockles, cleaned

½ cup torn basil

2 ½ cups canned crushed tomatoes

Salt and pepper

1. Bring a pot of salted water to a boil. Dump in pasta and cook 6 minutes for al dente.

2. In a large pot on medium high heat add chili flakes, Fresno chili, olive oil, garlic, clams and cockles. Season with salt and pepper, and cook until clams and cockles start to open. Stir constantly so that garlic doesn't burn.

3. Once clams and cockles start to open, add basil and tomatoes. Bring to a simmer and cook until all seafood opens. You might have to help the shells to open fully.

4. Drain pasta and add to sauce. Adjust seasoning and enjoy.

Fresh Egg Fettuccine with Manila Clams, Spicy Sausage and White Wine Saffron Reduction

These popular clams are delicious in this buttery sauce made with spicy sausages. The saffron turns it bright yellow, and the fettuccine ribbons are the perfect canvas for it. You can substitute littleneck or cherrystone clams for the Manilas—just make sure they are fresh.

Serves 3 to 4

10 MINUTES PREP TIME
20 MINUTES COOKING TIME

1 teaspoon red chili flakes
1 cup ground Italian sausage*
4 cloves garlic, minced
12 to 15 Manila clams
Pinch of saffron
1 cup white wine
1 cup chicken broth
1 pound fresh egg fettuccine,
see recipe p. 80
6 tablespoons butter
½ cup torn Italian parsley
leaves
Salt and pepper
Olive oil

1. Bring a large pot of salted water to a boil.

2. In a large pot on medium high heat, drizzle in a touch of olive oil. Add the chili flakes, sausage, garlic and clams and cook for 5 minutes.

3. Add the saffron and deglaze with the white wine. Cook for two minutes, then add the chicken broth. Adjust seasoning with salt and pepper. Reduce by half, about 3 to 4 minutes.

4. Add the pasta to water and cook for 2 minutes. Remove the pasta and add to clams. Continue to reduce sauce, stirring pasta to release starch to help thicken sauce. Reduce heat to medium, add butter and stir to create sauce. If too thick, add a touch of pasta water to thin out. Fold in the parsley and season one last time with salt and pepper, if needed.

FABIO SAYS

I like both sweet and spicy **Italian sausage,** and of course you can buy it just about anywhere. I also make my own by grinding a one-pound pork shoulder and then mixing it with onion powder, fennel seeds and chopped fresh garlic (and chili flakes for spicy sausage). I then divide it into small flat patties that fit in two-ounce plastic bags. These go in the freezer and will thaw in 10 minutes in cold water. Now you can cook them as patties or break them up for whatever dish you're cooking.

*You can buy seasoned ground beef, or buy linked sausage, crumbling it as it cooks.

Fresh Pasta with 20-Minute Sausage and Beef Bolognese Sauce

You could use another pasta with this sauce, but pappardelle is classic. Making the sauce for the pasta doesn't take much time, while making a classic Bologna sauce is a lengthy, complex process of layering vegetables, beef, pork, milk, wine and tomatoes. A lot going on. The trick for this quicker sauce is to cook everything rapidly on a high fire and then add sausage to boost the flavor. It will also help if you do *not* reach for the leanest ground beef. A little fat means a fuller-flavored sauce.

Serves 3 to 4

15 MINUTES PREP TIME
20 TO 25 MINUTES COOKING TIME

3 tablespoons extra-virgin olive oil

¼ cup grated carrot

¼ cup grated onion

½ pound mild Italian sausage, ground

1 pound ground beef, 80/20

2 tablespoons tomato paste

3 garlic cloves, sliced

¼ cup red wine

1 large can crushed tomatoes

½ pound fresh pasta, such as pappardelle, *see recipe p. 80*

3 tablespoons minced fresh basil

¼ cup minced parsley, with some reserved for garnish

Salt and pepper

Grana Padano cheese, grated, for garnish

1. Bring 4 quarts salted water to a boil in large pot.

2. In a large pot on high heat, add extra-virgin olive oil. Add carrot and onion and cook for 1 minute. Add both sausage and ground beef and cook until ¾ done, about 5 minutes.

3. Add tomato paste and garlic and cook for 2 minutes. Deglaze with wine and reduce for 2 minutes. Season with salt and pepper.

4. Stir in crushed tomatoes and reduce for 10 minutes on medium heat until slightly thickened.

5. Add pasta to water and cook for 2 to 3 minutes, stirring to prevent sticking.

6. Stir in basil, parsley, and pasta and season with salt and pepper. Add pasta cooking water, if needed, to loosen sauce to liking. Garnish with grated cheese and parsley.

Risotto-Style Orzo with Marinated Shrimp

Easy, easy, easy when you've shrimp on hand (frozen shrimp are okay) and a jar of roasted red peppers. You could roast your own peppers, of course, but the jarred are a lot easier. The Fresno chili gives the pasta salad a little kick—and yes, it's a pasta salad: Orzo is a kind of pasta, although in this recipe it's cooked like rice.

Serves 4

15 MINUTES PREP TIME
30 MINUTES COOKING TIME

1 cup diced yellow onion

2 cups chicken broth

1 cup uncooked orzo

1 pound medium shrimp, peeled and deveined, 31–40 ct.

1 tablespoon minced garlic

1 tablespoon chopped Fresno chili

½ cup sliced roasted red bell pepper

⅓ cup chopped Italian parsley

⅓ cup freshly grated Pecorino cheese

4 tablespoons butter

⅓ cup loosely packed chopped basil leaves

Grated zest of 2 lemons, for garnish

Olive oil

Salt and pepper

1. Coat the bottom of a medium saucepan with olive oil and heat it on medium high heat. Add onions and cook for 4–5 minutes or until softened. Season to taste with salt and pepper and then add the chicken broth. Let the broth come to a boil and add the orzo. Reduce the heat and simmer the pasta rapidly for about 10 minutes, or until al dente. Stir it once or twice.

2. Meanwhile, coat the bottom of a large skillet with olive oil and set on medium high heat. When hot, put the shrimp in the skillet and season lightly with salt and pepper. Cook the shrimp for about 2 minutes, stirring a few times. Add the garlic, chili, roasted peppers and parsley, stir to mix, and cook for about 1 minute longer or until the shrimp turns pink and is cooked through.

3. Add the shrimp and the contents of the skillet to the saucepan with the orzo and stir to mix. The broth will be reduced by this time and will coat the shrimp.

4. Lower the heat to medium and fold in the cheese, butter, and basil. Adjust the seasoning and serve, garnished with the lemon zest.

Crispy Pancetta, Sweet Peas and Pecorino Risotto

With the pancetta, shallots and garlic at the beginning of the process and the peas, cheese and butter at the end, this risotto bursts with flavors, all tucked into its creamy texture. Risotto takes time, no getting around it, but with some good prep and attention, this one only requires about 30 minutes from start to finish. Use Arborio or another medium-grain Italian rice—long-grain rice, such as Carolina or Uncle Ben's, isn't starchy enough—and then be patient. The trick is to gradually add a large amount of broth to the rice, but to do so in small amounts, just enough to barely cover the kernels each time you add a ladleful. The small measure heats quickly and is absorbed in short order so that you can add the next. Constant stirring moves the rice around so it cooks evenly and helps distribute the rice's naturally occurring starch that contributes to the risotto's creaminess. Hold off adding the cheese and other finishing ingredients. Stir them in at the end of cooking. Remember: patience!

Serves 4

12 MINUTES PREP TIME
30 MINUTES COOKING TIME

½ cup diced pancetta

2 shallots, thinly sliced

3 cloves garlic, minced

1 ¼ cups Arborio rice

1 cup dry white wine

5 cups chicken stock

4 tablespoons butter

¼ cup chopped parsley

⅓ cup pecorino cheese, grated

1 cup sweet green peas

Fresh parsley, chopped for garnish

Grated pecorino, for garnish

Salt and pepper

Olive oil

1. In a large pot on medium heat, render the pancetta until crispy. Remove pancetta and most of the rendered fat separately, and then sweat the shallots and garlic for 5 minutes with a drizzle of olive oil. Add rice and cook for another minute. Season with salt and pepper.

2. Deglaze with white wine and turn heat to high. Reduce completely and add half of the chicken stock. Reduce completely and add a ladle at a time after that. Stir to incorporate each ladle until rice is cooked to desired consistency, about 20 to 25 minutes.

3. Once creamy, add in the butter, parsley, pecorino cheese, and peas. Stir in on low heat, adjust seasoning, and add a touch of chicken stock if needed. Garnish with parsley and pecorino.

FABIO SAYS

When you steam or cook **rice** in a tightly lidded pot, the goal is perfectly cooked grains that don't clump. This is not always the outcome. Sometimes the rice on the bottom of the pot burns. If this happens, lay a slice of white bread on top of the rice for 5 to 10 minutes. The bread removes the burned taste. Be careful to avoid the burned layer of rice when scooping it from the pot.

Four-Mushroom Risotto with Parsley Salad and Sun-Dried Tomatoes

I'm a big fan when it comes to risotto. My wife? Not so much. I think she got sick of it during the early months of our courtship when I made risotto over and over and over again, thinking I was impressing her! You can add just about anything you fancy to risotto, which makes it a creative cook's dream. For this recipe, I rely on four different kinds of mushrooms (you could use different mushrooms or only cook two or three types as long as the amounts stay the same), and if you forget about the risotto part of the recipe, you're left with an exotic mushroom dish. You can't deny this is awesome!

Serves 4

10 MINUTES PREP TIME
20 MINUTES COOKING TIME

8 tablespoons butter, divided in half

1 large onion, finely chopped

½ cup torn cremini mushrooms

¼ cup torn oyster mushrooms

½ cup torn shiitake mushrooms

¼ cup sliced button mushrooms

½ cups Arborio rice

1 cup dry white wine

5 cups vegetable stock

½ cup grated Grana Padano

2 teaspoons white balsamic vinegar

¼ cup chopped sun-dried tomatoes

½ cup Italian parsley leaves

Salt and pepper

1. Melt the butter in 2 heavy saucepans on medium high. Gently sauté the onions in one until softened, about 3 minutes. In the other, cook the mushrooms until caramelized, about 6–8 minutes. Season lightly with salt and pepper. Turn off mushroom pan.

2. Stir in the rice to the onions and cook, stirring all the time, for about 2 minutes, until the mix becomes translucent. Add the wine and cook for around 6–7 minutes, until the wine is absorbed. Season with salt and pepper.

3. Add 2 cups of the stock to the pan and simmer gently until the stock is absorbed, stirring every minute or so to prevent sticking.

4. Gradually add more stock, a ladleful at a time, until the rice is tender, about 15–18 minutes. Adjust seasoning in the risotto with salt and pepper and add the mushrooms. Turn heat to low and stir in cheese.

5. In a small bowl, combine the vinegar, sun-dried tomato, and parsley. Use this as a garnish on top of risotto when served.

FABIO SAYS

Nearly all the **mushrooms** in the market are farm-raised, and I say "good!" Let's stay with farm-raised mushrooms, which are as full-flavored as wild mushrooms and **safe to eat**. Gramps might still forage in the woods for mushrooms, but what if Gramps makes a mistake? Why risk your health (or your life!)? Every year in Italy you hear about someone getting sick or dying because they think they know which wild mushrooms are edible.

FISH AND SEAFOOD

When you go to a seafood restaurant in Italy, especially if it's near a pier or on a harbor, you only have a couple of fish to choose from. There won't be ten or twelve selections like you might find in the United States. That's because we only eat fish when it's fresh, the "catch of the day." Italians don't even entertain the concept of frozen fish or vacuum-sealed seafood. We don't eat fish that was caught four or five days earlier, either. Can you eat a piece of fish that's been in your refrigerator for three days? Of course. But for fresh flavor, eat it on the day you buy it.

For the best quality, go to the fish counter and ask for whatever is fresh. And when you get the fish home, leave it alone. What I mean is don't embellish the fish with a lot of sauces and garnishes. Fish prep should be quick and easy with the goal of highlighting the fish itself. If you handle the fish too much it breaks down, and no one wants that. Of course, meaty fish such as tuna and swordfish stand up to more robust techniques, but even they should be handled with care.

The recipes here are for simple techniques. Each has only a few steps, which means you can avoid the headache and get right to enjoying a delicious fish dinner.

15-Minute Seafood Cioppino

Cioppino is nothing more than fish stew—and a pretty basic one at that. Although there are no rules about what fish to use, go for what is easy to eat. Avoid fish with bones, like herring, and instead choose squid, shrimp, octopus, clams or mussels. You could add some halibut, trout or cod, but don't go crazy. The trick is to know how long the fish need to cook, because believe me, there is a special place in hell for people who overcook fish. I like this with shrimp and calamari. They cook quickly. Easy.

Serves 2 to 4

15 MINUTES PREP TIME
15 MINUTES COOKING TIME

½ teaspoon red chili flakes

½ teaspoon saffron

3 teaspoons butter

2 shallots, sliced

2 leeks, trimmed, cleaned, and sliced

5 sprigs thyme

½ cup white wine

12 mussels, cleaned

10 clams, cleaned

1 15-ounce can whole peeled tomatoes, crushed

½ cup calamari

½ cup cream

½ cup chopped basil

½ cup large shrimp, 21–25 ct.

2 ½ cups seafood stock

Salt and pepper

1. In a large pot on medium high heat, add the red chili flakes, saffron, butter, shallots, leeks and thyme. Cook for 3 minutes, then season to taste with salt and pepper.

2. Next add the white wine, mussels and clams. Turn the heat to high and cook until wine has reduced, about 3 to 4 minutes. Once the wine has reduced, add the tomatoes and cook for another 3 minutes.

3. Finally, add the calamari, cream, basil, shrimp and seafood stock. Adjust the seasoning with salt and pepper, cover with a lid, bring to a boil, and reduce to a simmer. Cook for another 5 minutes.

Oven-Roasted Escolar with Pine Nuts
and Roasted Peppers

Escolar is a firm, mild white fish that once you try, you'll want to try again. This is a straightforward way to cook any fish with the texture of escolar: Sear both sides of the fish in a hot pan and then finish it in a hot oven. The pepper and herb mixture that's served with the fish can be doubled or tripled and kept in a lidded container in the refrigerator for a week or so, ready for when you next cook escolar or another firm-fleshed fish such as tuna.

Serves 4

10 MINUTES PREP TIME
20 MINUTES COOKING TIME

1 pound escolar, cleaned
by fishmonger

2 tablespoons olive oil

2 teaspoons paprika

1 yellow bell pepper,
cored and sliced thin

2 red bell peppers,
cored and sliced thin

4 large garlic cloves, minced

½ cup dry white wine

1 teaspoon chopped parsley

2 teaspoons
minced fresh thyme

10 leaves basil, torn

2 tablespoons sherry vinegar

¼ cup pine nuts

Salt and pepper

4 roasted lemons,
see recipe p. 254

1. Preheat oven to 400°F.

2. Divide fish into 4 equal portions. Pat dry and season with salt and pepper.

3. Heat two large sauté pans to medium high, one for the fish and one for the peppers. Split the olive oil between the pans. Lay fish in one. Sear on one side for 2–3 minutes, flip, and toss into oven to finish cooking, about 3–5 minutes.

4. Add the paprika and peppers to the other pan. Cook for 6 minutes, then add the garlic and cook for 30 seconds. Deglaze with white wine and reduce completely. Season with salt and pepper.

5. Add the parsley, thyme and basil. Cook for 2 more minutes and deglaze again with vinegar. Cook for another minute then toss in the pine nuts and turn off heat.

6. Serve fish with pepper mixture and roasted lemon.

FABIO SAYS

The number-one reason home cooks give for not cooking is that it takes too long. There is never enough time. But I've found ways around it by **prepping ahead of time**, and by that I mean prepping months ahead of time. I have two freezers in my house. One is a thirty-cubic-foot freezer that I use pretty much like everyone uses freezers, and the other is a basic chest freezer for my prepped foods.

The cioppino on page 121 uses both basil and shallots. I prepare bunches of basil leaves, wrapping them in damp paper towels and then stowing the filled towels in small plastic freezer bags. This keeps the basil nice and fresh for a few months. I do the same with chopped shallots.

Dry-Roasted Scallops with Caramelized Raisins and Cauliflower Gremolata

Scallops and cauliflower taste good together and both are easy to deal with, particularly the scallops. Buy them as fresh as you can, with a little tinge of pink. Avoid those bright white ones; they've been overprocessed. And the cauliflower can be fresh or frozen. You can buy frozen cauliflower or freeze your own by first cutting the head into florets and then stashing them in a freezer bag for a few weeks. To avoid sogginess, blanch the florets for two minutes in lightly salted boiling water before you drain, cool and freeze. When they are caramelized as they are here, there is no difference in how to treat the fresh and the frozen.

Serves 4

10 MINUTES PREP TIME
20 MINUTES COOKING TIME

1 pound cleaned jumbo sea scallops

2 teaspoons butter

1 head of cauliflower, cleaned and cut into small pieces

½ cup raisins

2 cloves garlic, minced

1 tablepoon olive oil, or more to taste

2 tablespoons balsamic vinegar

1 tablespoon finely chopped fresh Italian parsley

Juice of 1 lemon

Zest of 1 orange

Zest of 2 lemons

Olive oil

Salt and pepper

1. Rinse scallops under cold running water to remove any sand or grit. Drain them well and pat dry. Season with salt and pepper.

2. In a large pot on medium high heat, drizzle in a touch of olive oil and add butter. Once the butter has melted, add cauliflower and cook on medium high until caramelized, about 10 minutes. Add raisins and garlic to the pot and cook for another 5 minutes.

3. Set another frying pan large enough to hold all the scallops on high heat. Drizzle in 1 tablespoon of olive oil, or more to taste. Place scallops evenly in the pan, and sear on each side for 2 minutes. Remove from the pan onto a plate.

4. Deglaze cauliflower with balsamic vinegar and add parsley, lemon juice, orange zest and lemon zest. Season with salt and pepper. Cook for another minute, then serve with scallops.

FABIO SAYS

Caramelizing is a technique that brings out the flavor of many ingredients by concentrating their natural sugars with heat. It's hard to determine exactly how long onions, shallots, mushrooms, carrots, cauliflower or whatever takes to caramelize because your stove, your pan, your food will be slightly different from mine. Rule of thumb? The food will color a little, most of the moisture will evaporate, and the food will start to brown both around the edges and on the side touching the pan. At this point, you'll want to use the food or turn it to allow the other side to brown. Watch it carefully so it does not go from caramelized to burned!

Pistachio and Pine Nut–Encrusted Pan-Roasted Trout with White Balsamic Butter Sauce

I always seem to have nuts in the kitchen, and crumbling them to coat fish turns out to be a straightforward and very easy cooking method. You can use this technique on other fish, too—maybe halibut, sole or flounder, particularly if trout is too "fishy" for you. If you replace the trout, adjust the cooking time to match the fish you choose.

Serves 4

15 MINUTES PREP TIME
20 MINUTES COOKING TIME

2 egg whites

½ cup pistachios

½ cup pine nuts

¼ cup chopped Italian parsley

4 cleaned fillets of trout

1 shallot, thinly sliced

3 sprigs thyme

½ cup white wine

½ pint cherry tomatoes, halved

1 cup white balsamic vinegar

12 tablespoons butter

Salt and pepper

Olive oil

1. With a fork, beat the egg whites until combined. Place the pistachios and pine nuts in a food processor and pulse to fully combine but not pulverize. Fold in the parsley.

2. Season trout on both sides with salt and pepper. Using a pastry brush, brush flesh side of the fish with the egg whites, then press fish into the nut mixture. Repeat.

3. Place the shallots and thyme in a sauce pot with a drizzle of olive oil and cook on medium high heat for 6 to 8 minutes until translucent. Deglaze with white wine and reduce by half. While reducing, put a large sauté pan on high heat and add the tomatoes to it. Let char in the pan for 1 minute, then drizzle in a touch of olive oil and remove from the heat. Toss in the pan for 30 seconds, then remove from pan and place aside on a plate. Wipe pan clean and add another good drizzle of olive oil.

4. Place fish nut-side down and cook for 3 minutes. Flip fish and turn off heat. Remove from pan after 1 minute.

5. Add the vinegar to the shallots and reduce on high heat until slightly thickened, about 4 to 5 minutes. Remove thyme sprigs and continue to reduce on medium until reduced by ¾.

6. Turn heat to low and whisk in the butter 2 tablespoons at a time. Serve fish with butter sauce and cherry tomatoes.

Seared Shrimp and Basil Whole Wheat Penne with Ricotta Sauce

What a good summer dish this is! Citrusy and herby, delicious hot or cold. I make this with whole wheat pasta because it's a little more chewy to the tooth. It's more healthful, too, although that's not why I use it. The finishing sauce includes ricotta cheese, which absorbs the flavors of the other ingredients and pulls everything together. If you want, use the roasted garlic on page 255 instead of minced garlic for a deep, garlicky but slightly milder flavor.

Serves 3 to 4

12 MINUTES PREP TIME
15 MINUTES COOKING TIME

½ pound dried
whole wheat penne

1 tablespoon minced garlic

2 tablespoons minced shallot

4 tablespoons butter

6 tablespoons
extra-virgin olive oil

1 pound tail-on shrimp,
peeled and deveined,
21–25 ct.

½ cup lemon juice

½ cup seafood stock

½ cup white wine

¼ cup chopped basil

¼ cup chopped parsley

½ cup ricotta cheese

Zest of 1 lemon, for garnish

Salt and pepper

1. In a large pot of boiling salted water, cook the pasta for 6 minutes.

2. While the pasta is cooking, in a large pot on medium high heat put the garlic, shallot, butter and olive oil. Sweat for 5 minutes, then add the shrimp and turn the heat to high. Season with salt and pepper and cook for another minute.

3. Add the lemon juice, seafood stock and white wine and reduce by half. Add the basil and parsley, then add the penne. Cook together for 2 minutes until flavors have combined and sauce has become creamy.

4. Fold in the ricotta cheese, adjust seasoning, and garnish with the fresh lemon zest.

Grilled Shrimp with Basil and Orange Sauce

A simple and straightforward summertime meal of grilled shrimp with a sweet-and-sour sauce that complements it flawlessly. If you don't want to fire up the grill, pan sear the shrimp. And if you fall madly in love with the flavors of the sauce, make a little extra and use it to marinate the shrimp before you cook it.

Serves 3 to 4

10 MINUTES PREP TIME
20 MINUTES COOKING TIME

1 pound cleaned shrimp, 21–25 ct.

½ cup finely diced onion

3 cloves garlic, minced

½ teaspoon paprika

½ cup white wine

½ cup orange juice

½ teaspoon cornstarch plus 1 teaspoon water, mixed together

¼ cup chopped basil

¼ cup chopped Italian parsley

4 tablespoons butter

Olive oil

Salt and pepper

1. Preheat the grill to high. Soak bamboo skewers for 5 minutes and then place the shrimp on them evenly. Season with salt and pepper and set aside.

2. In a sauce pot on high heat, drizzle in olive oil and toss in the onions. Cook for 5 minutes, then add garlic. Cook for another 2 minutes, then add paprika and season with salt and pepper.

3. Deglaze with white wine and reduce for 2 minutes. Add orange juice and cornstarch mixture and reduce until slightly thickened, about 2 to 3 minutes.

4. Reduce heat to low and add the basil, parsley and butter. Cook until sauce has thickened with butter and season to taste.

5. Place shrimp on the grill and cook on each side for 2 minutes. Right before taking off, glaze shrimp with a touch of sauce. Use remaining sauce for dipping.

Broiled Balsamic-Glazed Sea Bass with Celery and Fennel Salad

I like a good-textured fish for this dish, and sea bass is it, although you could use tuna or another meaty fish. I love buttery fish, but sometimes you need something a little more substantial. The floral notes of the white balsamic are great with the fish and in the accompanying salad. In this recipe, I sear the fish on top of the stove and then finish it under the broiler, but if you'd rather, increase the cooking time by 50 percent and cook the fish completely on top of the stove. If you have a fishmonger, ask him to scale the sea bass but leave the skin in place so it gets nice and crispy. If not, buy fillets, which are easier to cook.

Serves 2

10 MINUTES PREP TIME
10 MINUTES COOKING TIME

2 fillets striped sea bass, scales and bones removed

1 tablespoon chopped chives

1 tablespoon chopped Italian parsley

1 teaspoon dried thyme

1 teaspoon white balsamic vinegar

¼ cup baby spinach

¼ cup celery leaves

⅓ cup shaved fennel

2 tablespoons aged balsamic vinegar

Salt and pepper

Olive oil

1. Preheat broiler to high.

2. Season fish on both sides with salt and pepper. Mix the chives, parsley and thyme together in a bowl, then season the flesh side of fish with the mixture.

3. Heat a large nonstick pan to medium high, drizzle in olive oil, then place the fish in skin side down. Cook for 1 minute, then place in the oven to broil. Cook fish, checking to ensure it doesn't burn, for 2 minutes.

4. While fish is cooking, mix the white balsamic vinegar, spinach, celery leaves and fennel in a bowl with a touch of olive oil and salt and pepper. This is the salad to be served alongside the fish.

5. Remove fish from the oven and, with a brush or spoon, glaze with aged balsamic. Place back in the oven to broil for about a minute. Remove and enjoy.

Fennel-Crusted Salmon with Creamy Polenta

The salmon is nicely seasoned with potent fennel seeds and garlic powder before it's cooked to give it the strength it needs to stand up to the creamy polenta. Once both are paired on the plate, their flavors favor each other for a wonderful, rich dish. If you'd rather, use halibut or cod instead of salmon.

Serves 4

10 MINUTES PREP TIME
20 MINUTES COOKING TIME

4 salmon fillets,
6 ounces each

1 tablespoon
crushed fennel seeds

1 tablespoon garlic powder

1 cup instant polenta

1 tablespoon sage, chopped

1 tablespoon rosemary,
chopped

2 tablespoons
extra virgin olive oil

4 tablespoons butter

½ cup heavy cream

½ cup Grana Padano cheese

¼ cup fennel, shaved

¼ cup fennel fronds

Olive oil

Salt and pepper

1. Preheat the oven to 350°F.

2. Season salmon with salt and pepper on both sides. Mix fennel seeds and garlic powder together, then season the flesh side with that mixture evenly.

3. Grab a sauce pot and place 3 ½ cups of water inside. Bring to a boil, then whisk in polenta.

4. In a large nonstick pan on medium high heat, drizzle in a touch of olive oil. Lay the salmon skin side down in the pan and let sear for about 2 minutes. Flip salmon and place the pan in preheated oven for 3–4 minutes for a medium doneness. After 5–6 minutes it will be fully cooked.

5. When polenta starts to thicken, add the sage, rosemary, extra virgin olive oil, butter and heavy cream and continue to cook. Cook until very creamy, about 10 minutes. Add the Grana Padano in at the very end and whisk constantly to incorporate.

6. In a small bowl, toss the shaved fennel and fronds with a touch of olive oil and salt and pepper. Use this as a garnish when plating the salmon on top of the polenta.

Clam Stew with Chardonnay Cream and Calamari Bruschetta

Here's an Italian take on American clam chowder. Garlic, onion, wine, potatoes, even calamari go in the pot with the Manila clams. Use another kind of clam if you can't find Manilas, and let them open in the broth. I like to spoon the fragrant stew over thick pieces of toast or dip the toast in the stew. Use the best bread, toasted until crunchy, for a seafood feast! The broth is so good, I've been known to drink it with a straw.

Serves 2 to 4

15 MINUTES PREP TIME
20 MINUTES COOKING TIME

2 tablespoons butter

1 medium onion, finely diced

2 celery stalks, diced

3 cloves garlic, minced

2 bay leaves

⅔ cup Chardonnay

2 cups chicken or vegetable stock

1 pound Idaho potatoes, cut into ½ inch cubes

1½ pounds Manila clams, cleaned by fishmonger

1 teaspoon cornstarch

1 cup heavy cream

1 cup zucchini, sliced into ribbons

1 cup cleaned calamari, cut into chunks and tentacles removed

2 lemons, zested and juiced

2 tablespoons chopped parsley

Toasted sourdough or ciabatta bread

Salt and pepper

Olive oil

1. Heat the butter in a large pot over medium high heat. Add the onion and celery and sauté until softened, about 6 minutes. Add garlic and cook for 2 minutes. Season with salt and pepper.

2. Add the bay leaves, Chardonnay, stock and potatoes. Bring to a boil, reduce to a simmer, and cook for 10–12 minutes until potato has broken down.

3. Add clams and cook for 3 minutes with the lid covering the pot. In a small bowl, mix cornstarch with cream. Add mixture to pot and cook for 2 minutes, still simmering. Once clams have opened up, stir in zucchini and let cook off the heat. Adjust seasoning.

4. While zucchini is cooking, heat a skillet to high heat. Drizzle in olive oil and add calamari. Season with salt and pepper, then cook for 2 minutes. Add half the juice and zest to calamari, as well as parsley. Serve on top of toasted bread.

5. When serving the soup, add a touch of juice and zest to each bowl for a bright finish.

FABIO SAYS

Is your **bread** going stale and getting a little hard? A stalk of fresh celery in the bag will restore its flavor and texture. Be sure to seal the plastic bag once you put the celery inside.

Pan-Seared Halibut
with Balsamic and Red Onion Sauce

When you cook balsamic vinegar in this sauce it's sweetly redolent, pumped up a little with red onion—which also turn tantalizingly sweet when cooked until they caramelize. Even better, the dark sauce looks cool spooned over the simple white fish. If halibut is not available, try cod or sea bass. Aged balsamic results in the best flavor, and having the patience to let the sauce reduce until syrupy will yield like rewards.

Serves 3

15 MINUTES PREP TIME
25 MINUTES COOKING TIME

2-pound halibut,
cut into 5–6 portions
by your fishmonger

2 cups sliced red onion

¼ cup aged balsamic vinegar

¼ cup chicken stock

¼ cup white balsamic
vinegar

2 tablespoons
rosemary, minced

3 tablespoons
granulated sugar

3 cloves garlic, minced

2 tablespoons butter

2 sprigs rosemary,
for garnish

Olive oil

Salt and pepper

1. Heat a large nonstick pan on medium high heat with a drizzle of olive oil. Pat dry fish, season with salt and pepper on both sides, and lay in the pan. Let the fish cook on one side for 3 minutes to develop an evenly browned crust.

2. While fish is cooking, in a large pot on high heat add a small drizzle of olive oil and the red onions. Cook down for about 10 minutes until onions are caramelized. Add balsamic vinegar, chicken stock, white balsamic vinegar, rosemary, granulated sugar and garlic and bring back to a boil. Reduce until syrup-like, about 5–6 minutes. Once reduced, stir in butter to melt into the sauce.

3. Back to the fish: While the onion mixture is cooking and after 3 minutes on one side, turn the heat to low and flip the fish. Cook for another 3 to 4 minutes. When you flip the fish, place sprigs of rosemary under it to perfume the oil and fish. Use the fried rosemary as garnish.

Pan-Seared Sole
with Roasted Garlic, Spinach and Chilies

My mom makes this dish in about five minutes; I need ten! We both put everything in a plastic bag and refrigerate it so the fish marinates while we do something else, but letting it soak for fifteen or twenty minutes at room temperature works fine and allows you to get dinner on the table quickly. The garlicky spinach with fish is classic and it takes only minutes for the spinach leaves to wilt in the pan.

Serves 4

10 MINUTES PREP TIME
20 MINUTES COOKING TIME

4 sole fillets, 8 to 10 ounces, thawed if frozen

1 tablespoon chopped oregano

2 tablespoons chopped chives

2 tablespoons chopped parsley

2 tablespoons chopped thyme

½ cup olive oil

Juice of 2 lemons

2 tablespoon chopped Calabria chilies

3 cloves garlic, minced

4 cups fresh spinach

1 tablespoon white wine vinegar

Lemon slices, for garnish

Olive oil

Salt and pepper

1. Pat dry the sole, then season both sides with salt and pepper. Let it marinate in the oregano, chives, parsley, thyme, olive oil and lemon juice for 15 to 20 minutes.

2. Heat two large sauté pans on medium high heat. In one, drizzle in a touch of olive oil and place chilies and garlic inside. Cook for 2 to 3 minutes, then add spinach. Continue to add spinach, as it will wilt when cooked. Season with salt and pepper. Add vinegar, cover with lid, turn off the heat, and let sit.

3. Meanwhile, lay the fish in the other pan, being sure not to crowd the pan. Cook on one side for 3 to 4 minutes to form crust. Flip and cook on other side until cooked through, about 1–2 minutes.

4. Stir spinach around and serve with fish and slices of lemon.

Polenta-Crusted Catfish
and Braised White Bean Salad

If we made this in Italy, we'd use sole or flounder rather than catfish, but here in America catfish is a lot more available and affordable. In Italy, you can hardly take a bath without stepping on sole, so we cook it all the time. Catfish is mild, so I brush it first with mustard and then coat it with polenta to give it good flavor and a crunchy texture. The bean salad turns this into a meal. We don't make fish and chips in Italy, so think of the beans as a stand-in for the chips.

Serves 4 to 6

12 MINUTES PREP TIME
20 MINUTES COOKING TIME

4 skinless catfish fillets cut in half lengthwise

¼ cup flour

½ cup fine-ground polenta (cornmeal)

¼ cup Dijon mustard

Canola oil

FOR THE SALAD:

4 tablespoons butter

½ cup minced celery

1 cup sliced red onion, some reserved for garnish

3 cloves garlic, minced

1 tablespoon chopped thyme

Juice and zest of 1 lemon

2 cans great northern white beans, drained

1 tablespoon chopped tarragon

2 tablespoon chopped parsley

Picked celery leaves, for garnish

Salt and pepper

Olive oil

Roasted lemons, if desired, *see recipe p. 254*

1. Preheat a Dutch oven to medium high heat. Add canola oil.

2. Season fish with salt and pepper, then set aside.

3. Mix flour and polenta together in shallow dish and set aside.

4. Melt 4 tablespoons butter in skillet on medium heat. Add the celery, onion and garlic and cook for 4–5 minutes. Season with salt and pepper.

5. Add thyme, lemon juice and zest, and beans. Cook for another 2–3 minutes. Fold in tarragon and parsley, and cover with lid off the heat. Adjust seasoning.

6. Once oil is hot, coat fish completely with Dijon mustard. Press polenta flour into fish to form a crust. Carefully place fish in to deep fry, making sure to not crowd the pot (2 or 3 pieces at a time). Fry fish until golden brown and remove onto a plate lined with paper towels. Season with salt and pepper while hot.

7. Stir beans again to redistribute all flavors and serve alongside fish with celery leaves and sliced red onion to garnish. Serve with roasted lemons, if desired.

Lavender Pan-Braised Swordfish
with Roma Tomato Sugo

You won't believe how good this swordfish is once it's brined in a vinegary mixture of sugar and dried lavender to lightly perfume the fish. To make the brine more intense, cut back on the water and marinate the swordfish in a plastic bag rather than a pot. Cook the swordfish carefully, because you don't ever want it to overcook. Finally, finish it in a tomato sugo—a thick, rich sauce.

Serves 4

20 MINUTES PREP TIME
20 MINUTES COOKING TIME

2 tablespoons distilled vinegar

2 tablespoons salt

2 tablespoons sugar

3 tablespoons dried lavender

1 lemon, sliced

1½ pounds swordfish, cleaned by fishmonger

⅓ cup olive oil

5 Roma tomatoes, cut into chunks

5 cloves garlic, chopped

½ cup torn basil

1 cup tomato sauce

2 tablespoons chopped chives

¼ cup chopped Italian parsley

Salt and pepper

Olive oil

1. Combine vinegar, salt, sugar, lavender and lemon with 3 cups water in a pot and bring to a boil. Cook for 1 minute, then cool down. Once cooled, place into a large container with the fish. Let brine for 12 minutes, then remove and pat dry.

2. While fish is brining, place a large pan on high heat. Add olive oil and tomatoes to pan. Cook for 10 minutes while stirring constantly to break tomatoes down. Add garlic and cook for 2 minutes. Toss in the basil and tomato sauce. Bring to a boil, then reduce to a simmer.

3. Season fish with salt and pepper, chives and parsley. Heat a large pan with a drizzle of olive oil and lay in to sear. Sear on each side for 1–2 minutes.

4. Once seared, transfer fish to tomato sauce and simmer. Cook fish for another 5 minutes on low heat with a lid on the pan.

Lemon-Roasted Salmon Fillet with Creamy Pink Peppercorn and Brandy Sauce

Pairing salmon with a pepper-corn-brandy sauce is a good way to make it "not boring." Everyone eats a lot of salmon these days—something I like to see as long as the fish is good. Unfortunately, about 90 percent of the salmon in the stores is not worth it. It's farm-raised and has added coloring. Remember that salmon is not naturally red but is just pink, or *pinkish*, and its color is not uniform all the way through. Look for fish that is wild-caught, if possible, and that is more white than pink. Sure, you'll pay a little more, but the fish will taste better. If that means you eat salmon a little less often, you'll still be happy.

Serves 4

10 MINUTES PREP TIME
20 MINUTES COOKING TIME

FOR THE SALMON:

4 fillets of salmon, 5 to 6 ounces each

Zest of 1 lemon

Salt and pepper

Olive oil

FOR THE SAUCE:

½ cup pink peppercorns

1 lemon, cut into ¼-inch slices (you can use the lemon you zested if you want)

1 teaspoon thyme, stems removed

2 tablespoons minced shallot

2 cloves garlic, cut in half

¼ cup brandy

¼ cup chicken stock

8 tablespoons butter

Olive oil

1. Soak the peppercorns in water overnight to remove some of the harshness.

2. Pat dry fish and season with lemon zest and salt and pepper. Heat a large sauté pan on medium high and drizzle some olive oil inside. Lay in salmon flesh side down and cook for 2 to 3 minutes. Flip over and cook for another 2 to 3 minutes.

3. While fish is cooking, drizzle some olive oil in a large nonstick pan. When oil is hot and almost smoking, sear lemon slices for 1 minute without moving. (Regulate the heat so that the oil doesn't burn.) Then add the thyme, shallot, peppercorns and garlic, and cook for 1 minute.

4. Deglaze with brandy and chicken stock and cook until reduced by half, about 5 minutes. Reduce heat to medium low and incorporate the butter, while whisking, 1 tablespoon at a time.

5. Remove lemon slices and peppercorns with a slotted spoon, then place remaining contents of pan in a blender and blend until smooth.

6. Return lemon slices and peppercorns to sauce, stir, and pour over the salmon.

Grilled Sea Bass with Red Pepper and Pistachio Gremolata and Mascarpone Sauce

When it comes to firm, meaty fish, sea bass is one of my all-time favorites. If simply grilled until the outside is a little crispy and the interior sweet and flaky, it's just right for a rich, pistachio gremolata and a creamy mascarpone finishing sauce. The pistachios may surprise you (what are they doing in the parsley-based sauce?), but once you experience the texture and touch of sweetness they impart . . . magic!

Serves 4

15 MINUTES PREP TIME
10 MINUTES COOKING TIME

4 sea bass fillets, skin on

2 tablespoons lemon juice

2 tablespoons orange juice

2 tablespoons
red wine vinegar

¼ cup panko breadcrumbs

¼ cup parsley, chopped

¼ cup pistachios, chopped

½ cup roasted red bell
peppers, minced

Zest of two lemons, oranges,
and limes

3 cloves garlic, grated on
microplane

4 tablespoons butter

¼ cup heavy cream

¼ cup mascarpone cheese

Salt and pepper

Olive oil

Cooking spray

1. Pat dry fish, season with salt and pepper, and spray flesh side of fish with cooking spray. Clean grill to ensure grill marks.

2. Combine lemon and orange juice, vinegar, breadcrumbs, parsley, pistachios, bell peppers, citrus zest and garlic. Season with salt and pepper. Add olive oil until mixture just starts to loosen up, about ½ cup.

3. Heat grill to high and lay fish down. Cook on flesh side for 2–3 minutes, rotating a quarter turn midway through for hatch marks. Flip and cook for another minute, then remove.

4. Add butter, cream, mascarpone and salt to a pot. Cook on high heat and reduce until creamy, about 4 to 5 minutes. Serve on the table family style or, if you prefer, plate individual servings.

Brown Butter Sole with Fresh Herb Salad

Talk about easy! This is a perfect way to cook tender fillet of sole or any mild, white fish. Once the fish is lifted from the pan, a few more ingredients are added for a delicious almond sauce, then the fish is topped with a simple salad of fresh herbs and orange juice. Use your favorite herbs or whatever are freshest.

Serves 4

10 MINUTES PREP TIME
15 MINUTES COOKING TIME

4 sole fillets

4 tablespoons butter

¼ cup fresh lemon juice

½ cup shaved almonds

2 tablespoons orange juice

¼ cup olive oil

¼ cup torn fresh basil

¼ cup torn fresh
Italian parsley

½ cup arugula

Zest of 2 lemons

Salt and pepper

1. Season fish with salt and pepper.

2. In a large skillet over medium heat, sauté fillets in 2 tablespoons butter until the fish is lightly browned. Remove fillets and place in a warmed serving dish.

3. Add the remaining butter and cook until lightly browned, about 2 minutes. Stir in the lemon juice and almonds.

4. When the almonds start to take on color, pour the sauce over the fish.

5. In a small bowl, toss together orange juice, olive oil, basil, parsley, arugula and lemon zest. Season with salt and pepper and serve on top of and alongside sole.

Baby Spinach and Roasted Endive Salad with Pan-Roasted Shrimp and Lemon Dressing

A smooth, lemony dressing crowns this simple shrimp dish. If you like shrimp—and who doesn't?—you'll come back to this time and again. And once you discover there's a little bacon underlying the other flavors, you'll make it even more often.

Serves 4

15 MINUTES PREP TIME
25 MINUTES COOKING TIME

1 cup arugula

3 cups baby spinach, washed and dried

6 slices thick-cut bacon, diced

4 Belgian endives, halved

½ pound shrimp, cleaned, 21–25 ct.

½ pint yellow cherry tomatoes

2 teaspoons Dijon mustard

1 tablespoon red wine vinegar

2 tablespoons lemon juice

2 garlic cloves, grated

¼ cup extra virgin olive oil

Salt and pepper

1. Combine the arugula and spinach in a large bowl.

2. Heat a skillet to medium and toss in bacon. Render until crispy and remove.

3. Keeping some of the fat in the skillet and raising heat to medium high, lay in the endives cut-side down. Cook for 2 minutes, season with salt and pepper, and add shrimp. Cook for another minute, and then add tomatoes. Cook for another two minutes then pull off the heat. Adjust seasoning.

4. Add bacon back to mix and place in the fridge to cool slightly. Meanwhile, take the Dijon mustard, red wine vinegar, lemon juice and garlic and place in a blender. While on high speed, add a steady stream of extra virgin olive oil to create dressing. Adjust seasoning.

5. Once cooled, toss mixture and dressing with greens in large bowl. Be careful not to over-dress the salad.

Clams, Mussels and Italian Sausage in Prosecco Broth

If you like shellfish as much as I do, you will love the opportunity to combine clams and mussels in a buttery, creamy broth that is rocked with sparkling prosecco. And did I mention that sausage—hot or sweet, your choice!—turns this one-pot meal into a feast?

Serves 3 to 4

10 MINUTES PREP TIME
10 MINUTES COOKING TIME

2 tablespoons garlic, minced

3 tablespoons butter

1 shallot, minced

1 cup Italian sausage, raw

1 tablespoon oregano, dried

2 bay leaves

15 clams, cleaned

15 mussels, cleaned

1 cup prosecco

½ cup cream

1 cup chicken stock

½ cup parsley

Salt and pepper

1. In a large pot on medium high heat, add garlic, butter and shallots. Cook for 3 minutes, then add sausage and cook for another 2 minutes. Add oregano, bay leaves, clams and mussels. Cook for 5 minutes more.

2. Add prosecco and reduce by half. Add cream and stock, bring to a boil, lower to a simmer and cook until slightly thickened, about 4 to 5 minutes.

3. Fold in parsley and adjust seasoning with salt and pepper. Serve with grilled bread if available.

My best advice when it comes to buying meat is to make friends with a butcher, or even the guy behind the meat counter in the supermarket. This way, when you're in the mood for meat, ask him what's good or say, "I'm in the mood for a pork chop. Have any good ones?" There are rules to buying meat, and the butcher will help you follow them. For instance, fat means flavor, and you can't expect to get the same satisfaction from a cut of meat from the foreshank of the animal as you can from better cuts. There are ways to cook these "lesser cuts," but you have to know how. The recipes here and the butcher can help you.

In Italy, meat is a big part of our cuisine. We eat it all—even horse meat (well, I don't eat horse, but some people do). The dishes you'll find in restaurants and even in people's homes usually reflect the cooking style of that town, city or region, and if you're lucky enough to be in a private home, you can be sure the meat on your plate was bought at a local store. We don't have the vast displays of meat like Americans find in their supermarkets—we have butchers instead. I've found that the meat in American markets is pretty good: a fair average, I'd say. But it isn't the dry, aged beef or succulent pork you can find in a butcher shop or behind the meat counter at a specialty store. Ask your new friend there what to buy, and you'll end up with a better meal.

Chicken is popular in the United States, but the problem I have with it is that it's not very good. Sure, you can get good chicken here, but you have to look. I suggest buying it from a butcher shop where you can talk to the butcher, or if you shop in a supermarket, spend a few extra dollars for the best chicken they have. It's worth it not to buy birds full of antibiotics and hormones. Go for chickens that are free of antibiotics and have been raised "cage-free" and fed organic food.

In Italy, the chickens run free, or a lot of them do. My mom's chickens wander in the hills above Florence, returning to the coop when it gets dark. She feeds them table scraps and they forage outside for insects and worms or whatever it is that chickens eat. When it's our turn to eat them, they taste amazing!

So, look for a reputable shop where you can get good chickens. You will taste and feel the difference every time.

Pan-Seared Veal with Sage and Brown Butter Oven-Roasted Squash

A straightforward recipe for some nice, meaty veal chops. I usually buy at least twice as much meat as I need, season all of it, then freeze half to cook later. This method is so easy and delicious, I would probably cook these chops twice in the same month, especially when butternut squash is at its best in the fall. The squash, too, freezes well after it's been cut into chunks, and since you'll use about a pound for the two cups needed below, you might have some left over. Into the freezer it goes!

Serves 4

10 MINUTES PREP TIME
20 MINUTES COOKING TIME

4 veal chops, about 8 ounces each

2 tablespoons flour

2 tablespoons olive oil

¼ cup fresh chopped sage

2 cups cleaned, medium diced butternut squash

3 tablespoons butter

Salt and pepper

Lemon wedges, to garnish

1. Preheat oven to 400°F.

2. Put each veal chop between two sheets of waxed paper or plastic wrap and pound until thin, about 1 inch. Season with salt and pepper, and lightly coat with flour. Set aside.

3. In a large mixing bowl, mix the olive oil, sage and squash together. Season with salt and pepper and place onto a sheet tray. Put into the oven to roast for about 20 minutes.

4. In a pan on medium heat, melt the butter and cook on medium heat until golden brown, about 4 to 5 minutes. Remove pan from heat, but keep the butter in the pan so it stays warm.

5. In another large pan on medium high heat, drizzle in some olive oil and wait for it to just start smoking. Turn off the heat and gently lay the veal in to sear. Turn heat back on medium low. Cook on one side for 2 minutes, flip, then place pan into the oven. Let finish cooking for about 2–3 minutes.

6. Remove the squash from the oven. Place back into the mixing bowl it started in, leaving excess oil on the sheet tray. Pour in brown butter and toss completely. Serve veal with fresh lemon and the squash.

FABIO SAYS

Veal is an expensive meat that we ate only rarely when I was growing up in Tuscany. When my grandmother decided she wanted to cook veal, she'd offer to work a few more hours for the butcher she cleaned for—and in return he would "pay" her in veal. Most veal dishes in this book can be made with chicken or beef instead. They won't taste exactly the same—it's hard to capture the tender, mild, ultimately satisfying flavor of veal with anything but veal—but the final result still will be delicious.

The Best Quick Fried Chicken

I love fried chicken—and if you prep ahead of time, making it isn't the chore you might think it is. It's easy to marinate the chicken in the same butter-milk mixture you'll use when coating the chicken with flour and milk. I suggest cutting the whole chicken into ten or twelve pieces, as smaller pieces fry a little faster than large ones. I put the chicken in a zipped plastic bag to marinate the morning or night before frying, but even if you don't have time for that, be sure to let it soak for at least twenty minutes. Make sure the oil gets hot enough before you start frying, too.

Serves 4 to 6

**30 MINUTES PREP
AND COOKING TIME**

2 cups buttermilk

8 cloves garlic, crushed

1 whole chicken, cut into
10–12 pieces

10 sprigs rosemary,
divided in half

3 cups flour

1 tablespoon mustard
powder

2 tablespoons black pepper

2 tablespoons salt

2 tablespoons smoked
paprika

1 lemon, sliced

Oil for frying

1. Combine the buttermilk, garlic, chicken and half the rosemary. Let it marinate for 20 minutes in a plastic bag. Start to heat up the oil in a Dutch oven to 365°F.

2. Place the flour in a casserole dish and dredge the chicken, 1 piece at a time. Pour the marinade into another casserole dish and place the chicken back in the buttermilk.

3. Dredge the chicken back in flour again for a total of two flour coats and two buttermilk coats. Once up to tempera-ture, drop the chicken in the Dutch oven 2 to 3 pieces at a time so the pot doesn't get crowded. Repeat until all chicken has been fried.

4. Mix the mustard powder, black pepper, salt and smoked paprika in a large bowl and season the chicken with the mixture as it comes out of the pot. Take remain-ing rosemary and lemon slices and fry for 30 seconds. Remove and serve alongside chicken. Enjoy while hot.

Three-Pepper Chicken
with Roasted Carrots and Cauliflower

This is a Viviani family favorite, bursting with vegetables. It's so fast to cook and good to eat, you might make it one of your family favorites, too. It's a kind of smothered chicken cooked in one skillet that fills the kitchen with delicious aromas. Try to cook a pasture-raised or organic chicken, if you can. They taste better than others.

Serves 3 to 4

15 MINUTES PREP TIME
30 MINUTES COOKING TIME

3 chicken breasts, halved lengthwise

½ cup each diced red, green and yellow bell peppers

½ cup carrots, diced

½ cup cauliflower, sliced thin

1 teaspoon red chili flakes

1 tablespoon dried thyme

3 tablespoons white balsamic vinegar

½ cup chicken stock

2 tablespoons butter

2 tablespoons chopped parsley

Parsley leaves, for garnish

Olive oil

Salt and pepper

1. Pat dry chicken breasts and season with salt and pepper. Drizzle a large skillet on high heat with olive oil and sear chicken for 1 minute on each side. Remove and set aside.

2. In the same skillet, add peppers and cook for 2 minutes on high heat. Add the carrots and cauliflower, and carefully add a drizzle of olive oil. Let it cook for 3 minutes.

3. Add the chili flakes, thyme and another drizzle of olive oil. Cook for 2 more minutes, then add vinegar to deglaze pan. Cook for 30 seconds.

4. Adjust seasoning and cook for another 2 minutes. Take the chicken and tuck in-side the pepper mixture. Add the chicken stock, butter, and parsley and reduce to create the sauce for about 3 minutes. Once sauce is created, cover with lid and cook another 2 minutes off the heat. Remove the lid, swirl to incorporate all flavors, and serve. Garnish with parsley leaves.

FABIO SAYS

I make **chicken stock** in a pressure cooker, which doesn't take as long as more traditional methods and melts the marrow in the bones into the liquid for a rich, satisfying flavor—it's like other stocks on steroids. I ask the butcher for chicken carcasses to make the stock, and once it's ready, I freeze it so it's always available. This means we can have chicken noodle soup in our house in three minutes!

Brown Sugar and Rosemary Roast Pork Shoulder with Green Apple and Mint Salad

For me, a truly scrumptious dish is a slow roasted or braised pork shoulder or roast beef. Osso bucco is another. If you have fifteen or twenty minutes to prep and a little kitchen ingenuity, you can have a really special dish. The prep is intense, but once the pork is in the slow cooker, you can do something else. This isn't a braise; it's a dry roast, but the result is juicy and delicious. It melts in your mouth!

FABIO SAYS

The secret to saving time in the kitchen is to be prepared. Think about it: If you had ten hours to chop down a tree, it would be a good idea to take a good three or four to sharpen the axe. So keep your knives sharp, your pans clean and your pantry stocked.

Serves 4 to 6

20 MINUTES PREP TIME
10 HOURS COOKING TIME

2 pounds pork shoulder, trimmed of excess fat and cut into large chunks

¼ cup apple cider vinegar

½ cup diced celery

½ cup diced carrots

½ cup brown sugar

½ cup chopped fresh rosemary

2 ½ cups chicken stock

1 small onion, quartered

5 sprigs thyme

¼ cup arugula

¼ cup celery leaves

¼ cup whole Italian parsley leaves

½ cup torn fresh mint leaves

1 granny smith apple, cored and diced

FOR THE DRESSING:

1 teaspoon honey

2 tablespoons white balsamic vinegar

¼ cup extra virgin olive oil

1 small garlic clove, grated

Salt and pepper

1. Season the pork liberally with salt and pepper and transfer to a slow cooker. Add the cider vinegar, celery, carrots, brown sugar, rosemary, chicken stock, onion and thyme. Cook on low for 8 to 10 hours or overnight.*

2. Shortly before the pork is done, toss together the arugula, celery leaves, parsley, mint and apple in a large bowl.

3. In a small bowl, mix the honey, white balsamic vinegar, olive oil and garlic. Drizzle over the greens and toss to mix.

4. Serve the pork garnished with the dressed greens.

* If a slow cooker is not available, follow the steps above, place in a large pot, bring mixture to a boil, and place in a preheated 325°F oven to cook for 4–6 hours.

Chunky Pork and Veal "Bolognese" Sauce

I couldn't write an Italian cookbook without a Bolognese sauce. This one, made with pork and veal, is leaner than the traditional sauce made with beef. It cooks really quickly, tolerates high heat, and is packed with vegetables. Toss it with pasta, or, if you're not in the mood for Italian, use it in shepherd's pie beneath the mashed potatoes.

Serves 4 to 6

10 MINUTES PREP TIME
30 MINUTES COOKING TIME

¼ cup olive oil

1 pound pork shoulder, coarse ground by butcher

1 pound veal shoulder, coarse ground by butcher

¼ cup shredded carrots

½ cup peeled pearl onions

½ cup diced celery

¼ cup diced zucchini

½ cup red wine

1 cup chicken stock

2 plum tomatoes, diced

6 sprigs of basil, torn

Salt and pepper

1. In large Dutch oven on high heat, add oil, pork and veal. Cook for about 5 minutes, then remove meat.

2. Add the carrots, pearl onions, and celery to the pot and cook for 10 minutes, making sure to deeply caramelize the entire mixture. Season with salt and pepper.

3. Add the zucchini and cook for one minute, then deglaze with the red wine. Reduce completely, then add chicken stock, tomatoes, basil and the reserved meat. Bring the sauce to a boil over high heat.

4. Reduce on high, stirring occasionally until chicken stock is reduced and sauce looks creamy, about 8–10 minutes. Adjust seasoning with salt and pepper.

Pork Chops and Broccoli
with Red Wine Onion Agrodolce

I butterfly the pork chops for this recipe—slicing them horizontally so that there are two thin pieces of meat—and they cook in minutes. I suggest four-ounce chops, but if you find larger ones (six or more ounces), you can butterfly them and serve two people with one chop. I like the pork medium, but if you prefer it better done, sear the chops for about two minutes on each side. Once you put the seared chops in the sauce, they will need another one or two minutes to finish cooking. The sauce is a classic agrodolce—a reduced sweet-and-sour pan sauce that is perfect with the pork.

Serves 3 to 4

10 MINUTES PREP TIME
20 MINUTES COOKING TIME

3 butterflied pork chops,
4 ounces each

4 tablespoons butter,
divided in half

1 cup sliced onions

1 teaspoon red chili flakes

2 teaspoons brown sugar

½ cup red wine

1 cup beef stock

1 cup broccoli florets,
cut in half

Olive oil

Salt and pepper

1. In a pan on medium high heat, drizzle a touch of olive oil. Season pork chops with salt and pepper and lay inside the pan. Sear on each side for 1 minute, then remove onto a plate.

2. In the same pan, add half the butter and melt. Then add the onions and turn the heat to high. Cook the onions for 3 minutes, stirring regularly. Add chili flakes, brown sugar and wine. Reduce this mixture for 2 minutes, then add beef stock.

3. When stock is reduced by half, add broccoli and the other half of butter. Place chops back into pan and continue to cook. Once sauce is reduced and thickened, about 4 to 6 minutes, adjust seasoning with salt and pepper. Serve while hot.

FABIO SAYS

If you pour a little cider or wine vinegar over **defrosting meat**, it will help the meat thaw more quickly while adding a little flavor and tenderizing.

Roasted Leg of Lamb, Applewood Bacon and Roasted Mushrooms

When you want to celebrate—you've bought a new house, your future in-laws are coming over, your kid is home from the military—nothing is better than a leg of lamb that's slow cooked until the meat falls from the bone. The applewood bacon gives the meat appealing smokiness and mingles with the pan juices on the bottom of the cooker. Be sure to scoop those juices up and pour them over the lamb when you serve it. This is a caveman meal if ever there was one—if the caveman had been a three-star caveman chef!

Serves 4

20 MINUTES PREP TIME
8 HOURS COOKING TIME

½ cup dried porcini mushrooms

¼ cup olive oil

1 leg of lamb, ask your butcher to cut it for you

½ cup diced onions

1 pound medium-diced applewood bacon

8 garlic cloves, cut into chunks

3 tablespoons balsamic vinegar

¼ cup marsala wine

2 cups chicken stock

3 fresh rosemary sprigs

10 juniper berries, crushed

Salt and pepper

1. In a small bowl, place mushrooms and 1 cup hot water to reconstitute. Heat a large Dutch oven to medium high. Season the lamb with salt and pepper generously, add the olive oil to the pan, and sear on each side for 3 minutes.

2. Remove the lamb and add the onions, bacon and garlic. Cook for 8–10 minutes, then deglaze with balsamic vinegar and marsala wine.

3. Add the mushrooms and their liquid, chicken stock, rosemary and juniper to the pot. Season to taste with salt and pepper. Bring to a boil, then pour into a slow cooker.

4. Place lamb inside slow cooker and cover with lid. Cook on low overnight, or start in the morning and it will be ready for dinner, around 8 hours.

FABIO SAYS

When I was ten or eleven, I learned how to **butcher meat** from the butcher my grandmother worked for, cleaning his shop. He gave her a whole lamb for Easter that year and I was fascinated as I watched him cut the carcass into the various cuts. I told him I wanted to learn how to cut up an animal, and he suggested I work for him after school and he would teach me. I took him up on the offer, and while I wasn't paid in cash, I always got a piece of meat to take home for Grandma to cook. I spent five afternoons every week with the butcher, learning a skill that I still rely on just about every day.

Homemade Pizza in a Cast-Iron Skillet

Pizza is pizza and cooking it in a cast-iron skillet ensures even, high heat for a good crust. You can have five or six skillets going at once, all with different pizzas and toppings. The frozen dough sold in the supermarket works well; I always have it on hand. It needs only a little stretching to work, no fancy rolling or spinning.

Serves 6 to 8

15 MINUTES PREP TIME
30 MINUTES COOKING TIME

1 pound store-bought pizza dough, thawed

2 tablespoons olive oil

1 cup tomato sauce

4 ounces fresh mozzarella, torn into pieces

¼ cup thinly sliced onions

¼ cup thinly sliced red bell pepper

30 slices pepperoni

2 tablespoons grated Grana Padano cheese

1. Preheat an oven to 400°F.

2. Take dough out of the fridge. Let it warm on the counter while you prepare everything else.

3. Divide the dough in half and roll out on a floured surface to be a little smaller than your 10- or 12-inch skillet.

4. Heat half the oil in the skillet on medium high heat, then place the dough in the skillet. Cook for 1 minute, then flip the dough and add half the sauce, half the mozzarella, and half of the onions, peppers and pepperoni.

5. Place in oven and cook for 6–8 minutes, or until cheese has melted and crust is golden brown.

6. Remove from skillet, sprinkle half the Grana Padano on top, and cut for serving. Repeat the process using remaining ingredients.

Beef Pizzaiola with Burrata and Peppers

When you flatten a piece of meat on the counter—using a meat mallet, a rolling pin, the bottom of a small skillet, or your hands—to arrive at uniform thickness and then roll it, it cooks quickly and the juices lock in. You could put some chopped rosemary and garlic in the center of the meat before you fold it over on itself, but you don't have to. Sear it in a hot pan and then let it steam in the sauce. I like to finish the dish with soft burrata cheese, which stretches nicely over the meat and veggies.

Serves 2 to 3

10 MINUTES PREP TIME
20 MINUTES COOKING TIME

1 pound flank steak, trimmed by butcher

½ cup small diced red bell peppers

½ cup small diced yellow bell peppers

1 tablespoon dried oregano

1 cup diced Roma tomatoes

5 cloves garlic, minced

½ cup tomato sauce

4 ounces burrata cheese

1 tablespoon minced chives

2 tablespoons minced Italian parsley

Salt and pepper

Olive oil

1. Using a meat mallet, rolling pin or the bottom of a small, heavy skillet, gently flatten the meat to uniform thickness. Season the flank steak with salt and pepper. Then cut the steak into 4 pieces, against the grain. Roll each piece, then hold each together with 2 wooden skewers. Heat a nonstick skillet on high with a drizzle of olive oil. Sear each side of each piece for 1 minute without moving. Remove from pan and set aside.

2. In the same pan, add a touch more oil, then the red and yellow peppers. Cook for 5 minutes until slightly broken down. Add oregano, tomatoes and garlic. Cook for another 5 minutes, making sure to break down the tomato. Season with salt and pepper.

3. Add tomato sauce, bring to a simmer, then place the steak back in the pan. Cover with a lid and gently braise for 5–6 minutes.

4. Tear burrata cheese into 5 or 6 pieces, stretch, then place evenly in the pan. Spread chives and parsley over the entire pan then finish with a drizzle of olive oil. Serve family style, with the pan as the centerpiece for the meal.

Basic Dry-Braised Pork

A roasted pork shoulder (also called pork butt for some reason) is great to have on hand for tacos, meat pies, pasta sauces, ravioli fillings—just about anything where nice shredded meat is needed. This is dry braised in a low slow cooker with only a little liquid, so you can't call it braised or, on the other hand, dry roasted. It's wet roasted. Use a Dutch oven or slow cooker—while the roasting takes a long time, getting it going takes only minutes. The vegetables, vinegar and herbs make it especially tasty. This also works for beef.

Let the meat cool to room temperature or use it immediately. If you'll be using it chopped, shredded or sliced, prep it now and refrigerate the prepared meat in a tightly lidded plastic or glass container. If you'll be freezing the pork, store it in a freezer-safe container or zipped plastic bag. Expel as much air from the bag as you can, and it'll be good for couple of months. Let the frozen pork defrost in the refrigerator. If you're adding it to a simmering sauce or pot of hot, cooked braised veggies, you can add it while it is still partially frozen. Be sure to label and date the container.

Serves 6 to 8

20 MINUTES PREP TIME
6 TO 10 HOURS COOKING TIME

2 tablespoons olive oil

2 to 3 pounds pork shoulder*

1 tablespoon black peppercorns

2 tablespoons balsamic vinegar

2 ½ cups chicken or beef stock

2 chopped carrots

2 chopped celery stalks

2 stems rosemary

2 stems sage

2 yellow onions, cleaned, quartered

3 bay leaves

Salt and pepper

1. In a large cast-iron skillet or Dutch oven, heat to medium high and drizzle in olive oil. Season pork liberally with salt and pepper, then lay in skillet to sear. Sear each side for 2–3 minutes, then remove from pan.

2. Place the pork in a slow cooker with peppercorns, balsamic vinegar, stock, carrots, celery, rosemary, sage, onions and bay leaves. Season lightly with salt and pepper and cover with lid. Set on low and cook overnight, or start in the morning to cook all day while at work or running errands. Use this pork for any application where you need quick braised meat for a delicious meal.

3. Once cooled, portion half into large chunks and shred remainder. Place in plastic bags and remove air from them to have pre-portioned amounts for any recipe you choose.

* You can also change the pork out with beef and follow this recipe step-by-step.

Braised Pork Shoulder and Roasted Vegetable Pot Pies

This pie is another reason I always have frozen puff pastry ready to go in the freezer. America loves pot pies, and this one falls in the category of one-pot wonders. It's satisfyingly filling yet never heavy; instead it's light and clean tasting, like a pot pie should be. If you have already cooked the pork, it's super easy. I use frozen vegetables here because why not? Easy, nutritious and guaranteed to cut prep time.

Serves 4

12 MINUTES PREP TIME
25 MINUTES COOKING TIME

1 package puff pastry, thawed

2 tablespoons olive oil

⅔ cup diced celery

1 onion, minced

2 garlic cloves, minced

1 tablespoon tomato paste

¼ cup flour

½ cup dry white wine

2 ½ cups chicken stock, or use beef stock for a darker color

2 teaspoons minced fresh thyme

1 ½ cups frozen pea-carrot medley, thawed

2 cups basic braised pork, cut into chunks, *see recipe p. 179*

Salt and pepper

1. Preheat oven to 375°F.

2. Roll out puff pastry and cut to fit whatever serving container you are using. Place on a sheet tray and put back in the fridge.

3. Add olive oil to a pot on high heat, then add celery and onion. Cook for 3 minutes, lower heat slightly, then add the garlic. Cook for another minute.

4. Add tomato paste and cook for 2 minutes. Toss in flour and cook for 30 seconds to incorporate with onion mixture. Deglaze with white wine, then add chicken stock. Bring to a boil, reduce to a simmer on medium heat, and cook for 5 to 7 minutes. At this point the sauce should be slightly thickened. Season with salt and pepper.

5. Add thyme, peas and carrots, and pork to sauce and stir gently to incorporate. Scoop mixture into serving containers and remove puff pastry from fridge to place on top of pot pies.

6. Place in oven and cook for 10 to 12 minutes, or just enough time to allow puff pastry to crisp to light golden brown. Serve immediately.

Prosecco-Braised Chicken with Sun-Dried Tomatoes and Leeks

Fresh and quick are two words to describe this chicken, made in one pot and brightened up with prosecco, Italy's much-loved sparkling wine. At the end of cooking, the sauce is smoothed out with butter and flavored with fresh herbs. I love how easy this is!

Serves 4

15 MINUTES PREP TIME
20 MINUTES COOKING TIME

2 pounds
boneless chicken thighs

1 cup flour

1 leek, white and light green parts only, halved and sliced thin

4 garlic cloves, minced

⅓ cup sliced sun-dried tomatoes

1 lemon, sliced

½ cup prosecco

1 cup chicken broth

5 tablespoons butter

2 tablespoons minced fresh tarragon

2 tablespoons chopped Italian parsley

Olive oil

Salt and pepper

1. Season the chicken with salt and pepper. Drizzle olive oil into a large Dutch oven on medium heat, enough to barely cover the bottom. Dredge chicken in flour on skin side, then place into oil skin side down.

2. Cook chicken on skin side for 1 to 2 minutes, then add the leeks. Cook for 3 minutes more, then flip chicken. Add the garlic and sun-dried tomatoes and season with salt and pepper. Cook for another 2 minutes and add lemon.

3. Deglaze with prosecco, then add chicken broth. Bring to a boil and reduce to a simmer. Simmer until liquid has almost reduced, about 5 minutes.

4. Once reduced, turn heat to low and swirl in the butter to complete the sauce. Add tarragon and parsley and adjust seasoning with salt and pepper.

Herbed Lemon-Roasted Lamb
with Cucumber, Pecorino and Dill Yogurt

Active prep time for this majestic dish is about fifteen minutes, and then you can leave it alone to cook for several hours until the meat is so tender it falls off the bone. I think of this as a meal fit for a king that you start in the afternoon so it's ready at dinnertime. Serve it with a cucumber-dill yogurt sauce, perfect with lamb.

Serves 3 to 4

15 MINUTES PREP TIME
2 TO 3 HOURS COOKING TIME

1 leg of lamb,
about 2 to 3 pounds
¼ cup chopped oregano
¼ cup chopped rosemary
¼ cup chopped sage
1 lemon, cut into slices
Olive oil
Salt and pepper

FOR THE YOGURT:
¼ cup chopped dill
¼ cup chopped parsley
½ cup seeded, diced small cucumber
½ cup grated pecorino cheese
1 cup Greek yogurt
Zest of 1 lemon
Salt and pepper

1. Preheat the oven to 325°F.

2. Prep the lamb by seasoning it with salt and pepper on all sides. Drizzle with olive oil and rub into the meat. Mix together oregano, rosemary and sage in a small bowl, then coat the lamb with the herb mixture.

3. Preheat a large pan or Dutch oven to medium high heat with a drizzle of olive oil in the bottom. Place lamb inside pan and sear on top and bottom for 2 minutes each. Transfer to a sheet tray lined with a baking rack, arrange lemon slices all over the lamb, and transfer to the oven. Cook for 2 to 3 hours, depending on the size of the lamb (a good rule of thumb is about an hour per pound). The meat should fall off effortlessly when done.

4. To make the yogurt: While lamb cooks, combine the dill, parsley, cucumber, pecorino, yogurt and lemon zest in a bowl, season with salt and pepper, and mix. Serve yogurt with lamb.

Braised Pork with Pan-Roasted Asparagus and Creamed Garlic Spinach

Asparagus and spinach like each other, and they both love pork, so go ahead and put them all on the same plate. Those big, fat asparagus spears you sometimes see in the market are great for pan roasting and taste wonderful with succulent pork; you can oven roast the big spears, too. I finish the meal with creamed spinach (made with fresh spinach, which I prefer to frozen). If you keep the flame high, the leaves will wilt faster than they release moisture, and you'll have perfectly cooked spinach in minutes. (And there's no squeezing excess moisture from a block of thawing spinach.)

Serves 6 to 8

20 MINUTES PREP TIME
6 TO 10 HOURS COOKING TIME

2 pounds basic braised pork, in large chunks, *see recipe p. 179*

4 tablespoons butter

½ cup diced carrot

½ cup diced onion

½ cup diced parsnips

1 cup chicken stock

4 cups spinach

2 cloves garlic, minced

10–12 jumbo asparagus ends, trimmed

½ cup heavy cream

Salt and pepper

Olive oil

1. Divide pork into 6 equal portions and set aside while sauce is made. In a large sauté pan on medium high heat, add half the butter, along with the carrots, onions, parsnips and a good drizzle of olive oil. Season with salt and pepper and cook for 10 minutes. Then add chicken stock, bring to a boil, and reduce to a simmer. Cook for another 5 minutes.

2. While those vegetables are cooking, heat two other pans on high heat with a drizzle of olive oil. Place the spinach and garlic in one pan and the asparagus in the other. Season both with salt and pepper. Cook spinach until wilted, about 5 minutes, then add cream and remaining butter. Bring to a boil and reduce until creamy and combined, about 3 to 5 minutes. Cook the asparagus for 3–5 minutes.

3. Take the pork and incorporate into root vegetable sauce until warmed through on low heat, about 4 minutes. Serve pork alongside creamed spinach and asparagus.

Chicken Pizzaiola with Smoked Mozzarella

Pizzaiola means "pizza man sauce" or something like that. I like to cook chicken in a sauce that tastes like the sauce you get on pizza. It's close to marinara sauce, but I add onions and black olives to enhance the flavor. The mozzarella provides layers of smokiness, and the onions sweeten the sauce so that you end up with flavor after flavor after flavor. If you have a pizza oven in your backyard, cook this over an open flame, or cover the sauté pan and let the cheese melt instead of sliding the pan under the broiler. It's all good.

Serves 4

15 MINUTES PREP TIME
30 MINUTES COOKING TIME

4 boneless, skinless chicken breasts

½ cup thinly sliced onions

5 cloves garlic, thinly sliced

2 Roma tomatoes, cut into thick wedges

½ cup black olives, sliced

1 cup store-bought or homemade tomato sauce

1 cup grated Grana Padano cheese

1 cup shredded smoked mozzarella

¼ cup minced Italian parsley

Salt and pepper

Olive oil

1. Season the chicken breasts with salt and pepper and then drizzle them with a little olive oil.

2. Heat a large, broiler-safe sauté pan on medium high heat. When hot, sear the chicken breasts for 1 minute on each side. Remove the chicken and set it aside, then turn the heat to high under the pan. Add the onions and cook for about 5 minutes, stirring, until the onions start to soften.

3. Add the garlic and drizzle it with olive oil. Cook the onions and garlic for about 2 minutes, stirring a few times. Add the tomatoes and olives and season to taste with salt and pepper. Cook for about 5 minutes or until the tomatoes start to break down.

4. Add the tomato sauce and bring to a boil. Reduce to a simmer and nestle the chicken breasts into the pan to finish cooking, 5 to 6 minutes.

5. Preheat the broiler.

6. Sprinkle the grated cheese over the chicken and top it with the mozzarella. Slide the sauté pan under the broiler and let the cheese melt and turn gooey. Serve immediately, garnished with parsley.

Oven-"Fried" Chicken
with Balsamic Chile Ketchup

One of my very favorites, sort of like grown-up chicken fingers served with ketchup and dressed up with balsamic, honey and Calabria chilies. The chicken is coated with panko breadcrumbs before it's "fried" in the oven. I'd never heard of panko when I was growing up in Italy—not surprising as it comes from Japan—but since we've been introduced, I use these crumbs all the time for their crunchiness. They're a little fluffier and puffier than ordinary breadcrumbs. Try them!

Serves 4

10 MINUTES PREP TIME
30 MINUTES COOKING TIME

2 pounds chicken breasts, boneless & skinless

1 ½ cups panko breadcrumbs

2 tablespoons minced rosemary

½ cup grated Grana Padano cheese

3 eggs, beaten

1 teaspoon black pepper

1 teaspoon garlic powder

1 tablespoon paprika

1 tablespoon salt

FOR THE KETCHUP:

1 tablespoon minced garlic

2 tablespoons honey

¼ cup aged balsamic glaze, *see note p. 8*

¼ cup minced Calabria chilies

1 cup ketchup

Sliced lemons, for garnish

1. Heat oven to 375F.

2. Cut chicken lengthwise to make thin breasts. Then cut those breasts in half to give you 4 portions per starting breast.

3. Combine breadcrumbs with rosemary and Grana Padano. Dip chicken into eggs and then press crumb mixture into chicken.

4. In a separate bowl, combine black pepper, garlic powder, paprika and salt. Then season breaded chicken with that mixture. Set chicken on a baking rack on a sheet tray and place in oven. Bake for 12–15 minutes, until chicken is done and golden.

5. While chicken cooks, combine the garlic, honey, balsamic, chilies and ketchup. Use this as your dipping sauce. Serve with lemon slices.

FABIO SAYS

Here's an idea for anyone who **"breads"** meat and poultry often. Buy yourself two lidded trays, each two to three inches deep and measuring about eight by five inches. Put flour in one, to a depth of about an inch, and the same amount of breadcrumbs in the other. This way, your breading station is ready and waiting for you. Sift the flour and breadcrumbs after each use, and after four or five times, toss 'em and start fresh. The food you bread will be cooked, so there are no worries about cross-contamination.

Pan-Seared Scaloppine of Veal with Roasted Ham and Smoked Mozzarella in a Chianti Wine Reduction

The veal is cooked similarly to pizzaiola—except there are no tomatoes! I sear the veal and then top it with ham and cheese, which as it melts creates a fantastic pan sauce. Make sense? The final reduced sauce is a glossy broth, neither thick nor watery. I like to team smoky, earthy Black Forest ham with smoked mozzarella here. The ham should be sliced paper-thin so that it almost dissolves into the veal.

Serves 4

15 MINUTES PREP TIME
15 MINUTES COOKING TIME

4 veal breasts, cut lengthwise in half

1 tablespoon flour

1 tablespoon olive oil

2 tablespoons butter

4 cloves garlic, minced

¼ cup Chianti wine

¼ cup white wine

⅔ cup chicken stock

½ pound black forest ham, thinly sliced, almost shaved

1 pound smoked mozzarella, cut into 8 slices

Salt and pepper

Minced parsley, for garnish

1. Preheat broiler to high. Season breast halves with salt and pepper and set aside. In a large pan on medium high heat, add the flour, olive oil, butter and garlic. Cook until flour has formed a blonde roux, about 1 minute. Add veal to the roux and cook on one side for 2 minutes. Remove from pan.

2. Deglaze pan with Chianti, white wine, and chicken stock. Season with salt and pepper; reduce by half, then add veal back to pan. Top with ham and mozzarella.

3. Place under broiler to melt and brown the mozzarella, about 2 to 3 minutes.

4. Remove from oven and reduce further, if needed, to form a creamy sauce. Garnish with minced parsley.

Lemon-Roasted Chicken
with Avocado and Warm Artichoke Hearts

This easy, fast dish embodies all that's good about pan searing with ingredients you're apt to keep on hand. The avocado and artichoke hearts are integral to the side salad for the lemony chicken, but because I warm up the canned artichoke hearts in the pan with the chicken, everything ties together. Warm salads are not too common in the United States, but believe me, they hit home when properly prepared.

Serves 3 to 4

10 MINUTES PREP TIME
15 MINUTES COOKING TIME

3 chicken breasts,
cut in half lengthwise

2 tablespoons lemon juice

1 small can artichoke hearts,
cut into quarters

2 heads frisee lettuce,
root removed

1 tablespoon honey

2 tablespoons
white wine vinegar

¼ cup olive oil

2 avocados, diced and pitted

2 cloves garlic, grated

2 green onions,
cut sharply on the bias

15 basil leaves, torn

Olive oil

Salt and pepper

1. Heat a large nonstick pan on medium high heat with a drizzle of olive oil inside. Season chicken with salt and pepper then place into pan. Cook for 2 minutes. Flip chicken and add lemon juice and artichokes to the pan. Cook for 2 minutes.

2. Pull frisee lettuce apart into bite-size pieces. In a large bowl, combine frisee with honey, vinegar, olive oil, avocados, garlic, green onions and basil along with warm artichokes and toss to dress. Serve chicken along with warm salad.

FABIO SAYS

You can count on me always to mean boneless, skinless **chicken breasts** whenever a recipe calls for chicken breasts, unless otherwise specified. They're easy to find and quick to cook, so why not use them whenever it makes sense? Keep a few packages on hand in the freezer for fast, nutritious meals.

Pan-Seared Pork Chops with Red Cabbage

Whether you call it red or purple cabbage, or whether you stick with the more familiar green, when gently cooked in the same pan as the pork chops, the cabbage transforms into the ideal accompaniment for juicy, bone-in pork chops. I like this best in the fall or winter.

Serves 2

10 MINUTES PREP TIME
10 MINUTES COOK TIME

4 pork chops, bone in

1 small head of red cabbage, sliced thin

3 shallots, sliced

5 cloves garlic, thinly sliced

1 teaspoon red chili flakes

2 tablespoons sugar

½ cup red wine vinegar

Olive oil

Salt and pepper

1. In a pan on medium high heat, add a drizzle of olive oil. Season chops with salt and pepper and lay into the pan. Cook on each side for 3 to 4 minutes, depending on the size of the chops.

2. Remove chops and add cabbage, shallots and garlic to pan. Cook for 5 minutes, until cabbage has partially wilted. Add chili flakes, sugar, and vinegar. Cook until liquid has evaporated and cabbage turns glossy, about 5 minutes. Adjust seasoning with salt and pepper.

3. Serve pork with cabbage.

DESSERTS

I talians are not dessert eaters, and Italy is not a nation of bakers. We leave that to the French, who, we joke, have to leave a lasting impression at the end of the meal to make up for what came before. (You know I'm kidding! I love the French!)

This does not mean we don't like sweets. It means I—and other Italians like me—lack the patience to wait by the oven for a cake to rise! We know baking is both an art and a science but not the art or science we feel the need to master.

The recipes I have selected for this chapter won't break the dessert bank of time, but they will satisfy your sweet tooth and relieve the boredom of a meal without dessert. And let's face it, desserts should be anything but boring and instead make you smile big time.

Brioche Bread Pudding with Strawberries

You can prep this in about thirty minutes, but don't forget it needs to cook and then needs about twenty minutes to cool slowly to develop the thick, syrupy texture that bread pudding lovers want, need, crave! At the restaurant, we microwave bread pudding for about fifteen seconds just before serving to make it a little sloppy. The strawberries topping the pudding almost turn into a jam as the pudding cooks, and the same would be true for whatever berry is in season. Finally, try to find brioche for the bread; a good challah also works well.

Yields
2 large ramekins

20 MINUTES PREP TIME
1 HOUR COOKING TIME

¼ cup maple syrup,
then more for topping

2 cups cubed brioche bread

⅛ teaspoon cinnamon

1½ tablespoons sugar

½ cup mascarpone cheese

¾ cup milk

2 eggs

Pinch of salt

1 cup sliced fresh
strawberries

1. Heat oven to 350°F.

2. Divide maple syrup and pour into the bottom of 2 large ramekins, then sprinkle bread cubes evenly inside. In a bowl, whisk together the cinnamon, sugar, mascarpone, milk, eggs and salt. Pour the custard over the bread cubes. Evenly spread the strawberries on top and swirl them into the custard a bit. Let stand for 20 to 30 minutes.

3. Place the ramekins in a roasting dish. Pour warm water into the dish so the water comes halfway up the sides of the ramekins. Bake until set and golden brown on top, about an hour. Leave the ramekins in the water, allowing them to cool for 20 minutes before eating. Drizzle with more maple syrup and strawberries on top, if desired. Serve warm.

Mascarpone Chocolate Pudding

A pudding that's almost like a mousse—what could be better? I usually serve this in small bowls because I don't especially like to share my food. Ever. But it's fine served family-style in a large serving bowl passed around the table. I think when you serve a satiny smooth pudding like this one, a little crunch makes it better, so how about some toasted walnuts? Not always, but sometimes when I crisp them, I sprinkle them with a little confectioner's sugar, both before and during toasting. Makes 'em sweeter.

Serves 8 to 12

5 MINUTES PREP TIME
30 MINUTES COOKING TIME

½ cup sugar

4 egg yolks

1 teaspoon vanilla, extracted from pods

¼ cup unsweetened cocoa powder

½ pound mascarpone

¼ cup marsala wine

½ cup whipped cream

¾ cup walnuts, toasted

1. In a large bowl, beat the sugar and egg yolks until light and fluffy.

2. Place the bowl over a saucepan half filled with simmering water, and whisk mixture until smooth and silky looking, about 1 or 2 minutes.

3. Still whisking, add the vanilla, cocoa and mascarpone. Whisk until smooth.

4. Slowly add the marsala, whisking constantly until the mixture thickens.

5. Remove from heat and spoon into pudding bowls, about ½ cup each.

6. Chill until set. Once set, pipe the whipped cream on top and sprinkle with the nuts.

FABIO SAYS

I love **mascarpone cheese**. It's rich, smooth, seductive, lusciously creamy and a perfect replacement for cream cheese and heavy cream. It's also one of the few cheeses that freezes well, because about 90 percent of its calories literally come from fat. It's not always easy to find and is usually sold in small tubs. Stock up when you see the tubs and keep them in the freezer. Let them defrost on the counter—they won't take long, maybe an hour or two—or in the refrigerator, and don't worry about the small pools of moisture that collect as the cheese thaws.

Orange Curd Parfait

I call this simple dessert a parfait because it looks pretty layered in a clear parfait glass, but it will taste just as good served in a ramekin or even a Mason jar. Making the curd is the hard part, but it's worth it—it tastes so fresh, rich and citrusy, especially topped with the pistachios and whipped cream.

Serves 4

15 MINUTES PREP TIME
25 MINUTES COOKING TIME

FOR THE CANDIED PISTACHIOS:

¼ cup sugar

¼ cup water

½ cup pistachios, unsalted

FOR THE CURD:

⅔ cup plus 2 tablespoons sugar

1 egg yolk

2 Meyer lemons, juiced and zested

4 navel oranges, juiced and zested

3 whole eggs

8 tablespoons butter, cut into small pieces

½ cup heavy whipping cream

1. To make the candied pistachios, combine the sugar and water in a saucepan over medium heat and cook until the sugar has dissolved. Stir in pistachios and cook until the liquid is almost gone and the pistachios have a fine candy coating. Remove from heat and spread pistachios to cool on a pan greased with butter or cooking spray.

2. To make the curd, whisk together the sugar, egg yolk, juice and zest, and whole eggs in a heatproof bowl. Set bowl over a pot of barely simmering water and stir mixture with a wooden spoon for about 15 minutes, until the mixture is thickened and you can draw a line across the back of your spoon and the mixture coats your finger. Remove bowl from heat and stir in the butter until combined. Strain through a fine mesh strainer. Chill completely.

3. Once the curd is chilled, whisk the cream until soft peaks form. Fold together half of the blood orange curd with the whipped cream.

4. Ladle remaining curd into cups, top with cream-curd mixture and sprinkle with pistachios.

Salted Caramel Chocolate Cake

If hot fudge wanted to be a cake, this would be it. Yes, it's a classic sponge cake, but a classic that is rich and chocolaty with hints of cinnamon, rum and espresso that bring home the indulgent chocolaty-ness of it all. I sometimes call this Butterscotch Chocolate Cake because after it's baked it's drizzled with a thick caramel sauce that's lightly salted. Sinful.

Serves 10 to 12

30 MINUTES PREP TIME
1 HOUR COOKING TIME

FOR THE CAKE:

1 teaspoon cinnamon

1 teaspoon nutmeg

1 teaspoon salt

2 teaspoons baking powder

2 teaspoons baking soda

¾ cup cocoa powder

2 cups sugar

2 cups flour

½ cup buttermilk

½ cup heavy cream

½ cup canola oil

2 eggs

1 teaspoon vanilla, extracted from pod

2 teaspoons rum

1 cup hot water

2 teaspoons instant espresso powder

FOR THE CARAMEL:

Splash of vanilla extract

1 teaspoon fleur de sel

¼ cup butter

½ cup heavy cream, plus 2 tablespoons

1 cup sugar

1. Preheat oven to 350°F. Grease and flour two 8-inch round baking pans. Set aside.

2. In a large stand mixer, combine the cinnamon, nutmeg, salt, baking powder, baking soda, cocoa powder, sugar and flour. Once combined, add buttermilk, heavy cream, oil, eggs, vanilla and rum; mix until smooth. Stir together the hot water and espresso powder. Pour slowly into the cake batter and stir until completely incorporated.

3. Pour the batter into the prepared cake pans. Bake for about 25 to 30 minutes, until baked through and a toothpick inserted in the middle comes out clean. Remove from oven and allow to cool down completely.

4. While cakes are cooking, combine the vanilla extract, fleur de sel, butter, ½ cup of heavy cream and sugar in a sauce pot. Bring to a boil and simmer for 5–6 minutes. Cook until caramel in color, then add the final 2 tablespoons of heavy cream. Stir for 20 seconds and let cool before glazing cake.

FABIO SAYS

These desserts are great, you say, but where are the pies, Fabio?

Let me explain.

I know how much Americans like pies, but I'm afraid I got my fill when I was a teenager and worked the overnight shift at a pie bakery outside Florence. I baked pies all night long, toiling in a sweltering basement kitchen outfitted with twenty double-decker ovens, each one hotter than the others (or so it seemed!). My job was to carry the unbaked pies from the bakery across an alley and down the stairs to the ovens—and then, once the pies were baked, back up to the bakery. And then take care of the next batch of pies. I did this for two and a half years, starting when I was fourteen, and earned about $2,400 a month. My family needed the income, so it was worth it, but let me tell you: To this day, whenever I see an apple pie, my back starts to ache and I break out in hot flash–like sweats!

Chocolate Peanut Butter Rice Pudding

This rice pudding is a little like a risotto because it's important to stir it as it cooks so the Arborio rice releases its starch for a creamy, dreamy pudding. When it's plated it looks sort of like oatmeal but it's a sweet, tempting dessert. And yet, there's no law against serving it for brunch or a weekend breakfast.

Serves 4

15 MINUTES PREP TIME
30 MINUTES COOKING TIME

3 tablespoons flour
3 tablespoons cocoa
1 cup water
½ cup brown sugar
½ cup uncooked Arborio rice
3 cups whole milk
1 teaspoon vanilla extract
1 tablespoon butter
3 tablespoons peanut butter
1 sliced banana, optional
Warmed milk, if serving hot

1. In a medium saucepan, whisk together flour and cocoa and slowly whisk in the water. Stir until most of the lumps are gone.

2. Add the brown sugar, rice and milk and cook, uncovered, over medium heat for about 25 minutes. Stir frequently.

3. When the mixture has thickened and the rice is cooked, remove from the heat.

4. Stir in the vanilla extract, butter and peanut butter.

5. If desired, slice a banana and stir in or lay slices on top of each serving.

6. Can be served warm with warmed milk poured on top, at room temperature, or even cold without milk.

Strawberry-Almond Soufflé

A soufflé that marries the subtle flavors of almonds from the amaretto with the boldness of fresh strawberries. Perfect balance.

Serves 6

1 HOUR PREP TIME
30 MINUTES COOKING TIME

1 tablespoon softened butter

⅓ cup sugar,
plus 2 tablespoons

1 pint of strawberries,
hulled and pureed

3 tablespoons amaretto

5 egg whites

⅛ teaspoon cream of tartar

1. Coat a 2-quart soufflé dish with the butter. Dust the dish with 2 tablespoons of sugar, then put the strawberry puree and ⅓ cup sugar in a saucepan. Heat until dissolved and stir in the amaretto. Set aside.

2. In a large mixing bowl, beat the egg whites until foamy. Add the cream of tartar and continue to beat until the egg whites will hold stiff peaks. Cover and refrigerate the egg whites for about an hour.

3. Preheat the oven to 375°F.

4. Heat the puree in the saucepan to simmering. Pour the hot puree into the egg whites while beating at high speed until incorporated.

5. Spoon the mixture into the prepared soufflé dish and bake for 25 to 30 minutes, or until the soufflé is golden brown.

SOUFFLÉ MAGIC

The hardest part about making soufflés is resisting the urge to fuss over them. Once they're in the oven, let them cook. No peeking. Soufflés inflate quickly and deflate just as fast, so the best advice I can give you is to beat the egg whites to the consistency instructed in the recipe, fill the soufflé dishes to the rim, and then pop them in the hot oven and walk away. When a soufflé is done, serve it right away. It will stand tall above the rim of the soufflé dish or ramekin only for so long, like a rock star's hair. Maybe this is why they're the rock stars of the culinary world.

White Chocolate Soufflés with Milk Chocolate Sauce

Elegant ramekins filled with sweet white chocolate are ideal for a dinner party. If you have small jugs or pitchers, fill each with the milk chocolate sauce so that everyone is in control of their sauce requirements!

Serves 6

10 MINUTES PREP TIME
20 MINUTES COOKING TIME

4 tablespoons butter, half of it softened

2 tablespoons granulated sugar

2 tablespoons flour

1 cup whole milk

9 ounces finely chopped white chocolate

1 vanilla bean, seeded

4 eggs, separated

¼ cup powdered sugar

FOR THE SAUCE:

⅓ cup heavy cream

2 tablespoons crème de cacao

5 ounces finely chopped milk chocolate

2 tablespoons powdered sugar

1. Preheat oven to 375°F.

2. Grease 6 soufflé ramekins with the 2 tablespoons of softened butter and then sprinkle evenly with granulated sugar. Melt the remaining 2 tablespoons of butter in a medium saucepan over medium heat. Add the flour and stir to combine. Cook for 1 minute.

3. Stir the milk into the butter-flour mixture and bring to a simmer. Remove from heat. Add the chopped white chocolate to melt, then whisk in the vanilla seeds and egg yolks. Transfer to a large bowl.

4. In a separate bowl, whisk the egg whites with electric beaters until foamy. Gradually add the powdered sugar, whisking until the egg whites form medium peaks.

5. Stir ¼ of the egg whites through the white chocolate mixture to loosen. Gently fold in remaining egg whites. Carefully spoon the mixture into the prepared ramekins and level with spatula. Place ramekins on baking tray and bake for 18 minutes until soufflés rise.

6. To make the topping: Bring cream and crème de cacao to a simmer in a saucepan. Place milk chocolate in a small bowl and pour hot cream over it. Stir to combine.

7. Remove soufflés from oven, dust lightly with powdered sugar and place on serving plates. Serve immediately.

Raspberry Semisweet Chocolate Pots

Anyone who appreciates the combination of raspberry and chocolate would be out of their mind not to love this luxurious, luscious dessert. The silky smooth pudding has to cool for a few hours before you can eat it, which makes this the perfect dessert to make in the morning for serving that evening.

Serves 4 to 6

10 MINUTES PREP TIME
2 HOURS INACTIVE TIME
30 MINUTES COOKING TIME

⅛ teaspoon salt

3 tablespoons cornstarch

⅓ cup unsweetened cocoa

2 cups whole milk

⅔ cup and 1 ½ cups granulated sugar, measured separately

1 egg, lightly beaten

4 ounces chopped semisweet chocolate

2 teaspoons vanilla extract

2 cups raspberries

2 tablespoons powdered sugar, if desired

Fresh raspberries, if desired

1. Whisk together the salt, cornstarch, cocoa, whole milk and ⅔ cup of sugar in a medium-size heavy saucepan over medium high heat. Whisk constantly for 5 minutes or until mixture is hot.

2. Gradually whisk ½ cup hot milk mixture into the beaten egg. Whisk egg mixture back into the remaining hot milk mixture.

3. Cook, whisking constantly, for around 3 to 5 minutes, looking for a thickened consistency. Remove from heat and add chopped chocolate to melt, about 5 minutes. Stir in vanilla extract.

4. Pour mixture into a glass bowl. Place heavy-duty plastic wrap directly on surface of warm mixture and chill in the fridge for 2 hours, until pudding is completely cool.

5. While cooling, place remaining 1 ½ cups of granulated sugar and raspberries in a sauce pot on medium high heat. Cook until fruit starts to break down, about 5 minutes, then turn heat to high to continue cooking for another 10 to 15 minutes until a jam consistency has formed. Cool completely.

6. To serve, spoon raspberry jam into serving containers, about 1 tablespoon each, then pudding, about ⅓ cup each, finishing with the remainder of the raspberry jam. Top with powdered sugar, and additional fresh raspberries, if desired.

FABIO SAYS

Even a smooth dessert like these raspberry-chocolate pots benefits from a little **crunch**. If you have pine nuts or caramelized walnuts in the kitchen, toss on a handful before serving. If you have kids, you might have a box of Cap'n Crunch cereal in the pantry. Try a handful of that on the pudding … oh my God!

Red Raspberry Pudding

Don't look for the raspberry to be a garnish; it's the body of the dessert, cooked with tapioca so that it resembles a jam and spiked just enough with wine and balsamic vinegar to provide the most tantalizing hints of those seductive flavors. I then layer it with crumbled-up Oreos. Who needs more?

Serves 2 to 4

10 MINUTES PREP TIME
30 MINUTES COOKING TIME

2 pounds frozen raspberries

¼ cup granulated sugar

3 tablespoons dry red wine

2 tablespoons balsamic vinegar

1 tablespoon tapioca

1 cup heavy cream

2 tablespoons powdered sugar

2 teaspoons vanilla extract

1 cup Oreo cookies, or other chocolate cookies, crumbled

Whipped cream, for garnish

Fresh raspberries, for garnish

1. In a medium saucepan, stir together the frozen raspberries, granulated sugar, red wine and balsamic. Bring mixture to a boil, stirring constantly. Lower heat, add tapioca and simmer, stirring frequently, for 20–25 minutes.

2. Pour pudding into a bowl and cool. Cover and refrigerate 8 hours or overnight.

3. Mix the heavy cream, powdered sugar and vanilla extract in the bowl of a stand mixer and whip on medium speed with the whisk attachment until thick, about 3 to 5 minutes.

4. Spoon ½ cup of the cooled pudding into each individual serving dish, and add a layer of crumbled Oreo cookies. Repeat layering process, ending with cookies.

5. To serve, top each serving with whipped cream and fresh raspberries, if desired.

FABIO SAYS

Italy has a good variety of **fruit**. As a boy, I remember eating a lot of cherries, peaches, apples . . . just about any fruit in season. It's the perfect way to finish a meal without cooking. Think about strawberries or raspberries drizzled with chocolate sauce or syrupy balsamic vinegar. Or how about lightly grilled peaches with a sprinkle of brown sugar and spoonful of whipped cream?

Baking is a science, not so much an art—although lots of desserts look like works of art. If you mess up a little making risotto or pasta sauce, not much will happen. If you mess up a baking recipe that uses yeast and flour, the recipe will fail.

Fresh fruit gives you a chance to have a sweet result with a lot less work.

Salted Caramel and Nutella Popcorn

This recipe has no history or lore. It's a bowl of old-fashioned popcorn mixed with two awesome sweet sauces. You're welcome!

Serves 2

10 MINUTES PREP TIME
20 MINUTES COOK TIME

2 tablespoons olive oil

1 cup unpopped popcorn kernels

1 cup sugar

½ cup Nutella

½ cup heavy cream, plus 3 tablespoons

4 tablespoons butter

2 teaspoons sea salt

1. In a large pot on medium high heat, add kernels and oil. Place a lid on the pot and allow the corn to begin popping.

2. While popping, grab two sauce pots. Fill one with sugar and the other with Nutella. Turn the sugar pot on medium heat and begin to caramelize sugar. Cook until golden brown in color, about 10 to 15 minutes.

3. Heat the Nutella pot with a low heat and add 3 tablespoons heavy cream. Cook and stir regularly for 10 minutes.

4. In the sugar pot, take off the heat and add the butter and remaining heavy cream, and stir to incorporate. Let cool slightly, then add sea salt.

5. Check on popcorn to ensure all the kernels have been popped. Serve both sauces drizzled liberally on top of the popcorn.

FABIO SAYS

I've been eating **Nutella** since I was a little kid. It was affordable, and my very young mom came to rely on it as a way to keep me quiet. She's told me that she sometimes stirred it into the milk in my bottle. When I was older, I remember her threatening to withhold the chocolate-hazelnut treat if I didn't behave. I behaved!

Spiced Chocolate Pudding with Toasted Rice Crisps

Here's the Italian version of Mexican chocolate printed in a book published in the United States. Talk about globalization! This cream-based chocolate pudding is spiced with cinnamon and anise, and its silken smoothness is topped with crispy rice cereal—crisped up in the oven or a skillet. This is followed by generous dollops of whipped cream enriched with condensed milk, which provides just the right amount of sweetness to the cream. Texture, texture, texture… flavor, flavor, flavor!

Serves 4

10 MINUTES PREP TIME
20 MINUTES ACTIVE COOKING TIME
3 HOURS INACTIVE COOKING TIME

½ teaspoon salt

2 teaspoons vanilla extract

4 cups heavy whipping cream

2 cinnamon sticks

2 whole star anise

5 gelatin sheets, soaked in cold water and drained

10 ounces roughly chopped bittersweet chocolate

3 cups crisped rice cereal

2 tablespoons sweetened condensed milk

1. Preheat oven to 400°F.

2. Place salt, vanilla extract, 3 cups of whipping cream, cinnamon sticks and star anise in a small saucepan and bring to a simmer using high heat. Let cook for 15 minutes on simmer. Remove cinnamon and star anise, then add the gelatin sheets and stir until dissolved.

3. Add the chocolate and stir until melted and smooth. Remove from the heat and strain through a fine-mesh sieve. Divide among preferred serving bowls and refrigerate until set, at least 3 hours.

4. While mixture is cooling, line a baking sheet with foil. Place rice cereal on sheet tray and cook until golden brown, about 6 to 8 minutes.

5. Whisk the condensed milk and remaining 1 cup of cream in a stand mixer until medium peaks form. Serve cream on top of puddings and sprinkle with rice cereal.

DOWN TO BASICS

I didn't quite know what to name this chapter. Basics? Extras? Embellishments? Whatever it's called, it's packed with recipes for butters, vinaigrettes and other things that turn ordinary recipes into special ones. These are the items you sprinkle, drizzle, spoon and spread on food to give it pizzazz, and that let you build on the foundation of a dish so you can make it your own.

FABIO SAYS

Vinaigrettes are always thought of as mostly oil and vinegar. That's the classic definition, but while a good vinegar mixed with a good olive oil produces a good dressing, vinaigrettes can be so much more—almost a composed sauce that, when used to dress a salad, becomes more than just the seasoning. When you add shallots and a generous amount of parsley to a vinaigrette, for instance, the dressing takes the salad to a new height.

Some ingredients for vinaigrettes are cooked before they're added to the vin. Take a look at the recipes for Blistered Tomato Dressing with Basil and Pepperoncini and Roasted Apricot Dressing. The ingredients might surprise you at first, but imagine them tossed with lettuces and crisp vegetables, and your mouth will start to water.

I like to make more vinaigrette than I need and keep it at the ready in the refrigerator. The vinaigrettes in this book easily last a week, and if you freeze them, they last for a month. Yes. They will freeze. Oil freezes, although perhaps not as solidly as butter. Freeze small amounts of vinaigrettes—in an ice tray, maybe—so you can use all of what you defrost.

Parsley, Lemon and Thyme Vinaigrette

**Yields about
2 cups dressing**

5 MINUTES PREP TIME

1 teaspoon ground coriander

1 teaspoon honey

2 tablespoons
fresh lime juice

2 tablespoons fresh thyme

2 tablespoons minced shallot

¼ cup fresh lemon juice

¼ cup chopped
Italian parsley

1 small garlic clove, grated

¾ cup extra virgin olive oil

Salt and pepper

1. Combine the coriander, honey, lime juice, thyme, shallot, lemon juice, parsley and garlic in a blender and pulse 4 times. Season with salt and pepper, and add the oil.

2. Blend on high speed for 1 minute until dressing is fully combined. Adjust seasoning with salt and pepper.

Dill, Cucumber and Tarragon Vinaigrette

Yields about 2 cups

5 MINUTES PREP TIME

½ teaspoon pepper

1 teaspoon salt

2 teaspoons Dijon mustard

1 tablespoon fresh dill

1 tablespoon fresh tarragon

2 tablespoons minced shallot

3 tablespoons
white balsamic vinegar

½ cup diced and seeded
cucumber

1 cup extra-virgin olive oil

1 small garlic clove, peeled

Combine the pepper, salt, Dijon mustard, dill, tarragon, shallots, white balsamic vinegar, cucumber, extra-virgin olive oil, and garlic in a blender. Pulse 5 times then blend continuously for 1 minute. Adjust seasoning with salt and pepper if needed.

Blistered Tomato Vinaigrette with Basil and Pepperoncini

Yields 4 servings

10 MINUTES PREP TIME
12 MINUTES COOKING TIME

2 pints heirloom cherry tomatoes, halved

1 tablespoon butter

⅓ cup olive oil

½ cup thinly sliced pepperoncini

5 cloves garlic, sliced thin

2 tablespoons pepperoncini liquid

2 tablespoons white wine vinegar

½ cup chopped basil

Salt and pepper

1. Place a large skillet on high heat. Add the tomatoes and let them cook for 1 minute, charring on the outside. Turn off heat, then add butter and olive oil. When butter has melted, turn heat back on, high.

2. Add the pepperoncini and garlic, and cook for 4–5 minutes, while breaking tomatoes down to form a sauce.

3. Next, add the pepperoncini liquid and vinegar to the pan. Let reduce for 1 minute, then add the basil. Cook for another minute and adjust seasoning with salt and pepper.

Roasted Apricot Dressing

Yields about 3 ½ cups

15 MINUTES PREP TIME

2 cups store-bought, dried apricots

2 teaspoons fresh thyme

2 teaspoons stone ground mustard

2 tablespoons minced shallots

¼ cup champagne vinegar

½ cup orange juice

1 garlic clove, minced

½ cup olive oil

1 cup extra-virgin olive oil

Salt and pepper

1. Preheat oven to 400°F.

2. Place the apricots on a sheet tray with a drizzle of olive oil and place in the oven for 10 minutes.

3. Once apricots are roasted, add the thyme, mustard, shallots, vinegar, orange juice and garlic into a blender. Season with salt and pepper, then pulse 3 times. Add the roasted apricots and turn blender on full speed. Blend for 1 minute, then stream in both oils to emulsify the dressing, another 2 minutes or so.

Roasted Lemon Vinaigrette

Yields about 2 cups

5–10 MINUTES PREP TIME

4 lemons, halved

2 teaspoons Dijon mustard

2 teaspoons
fresh Italian parsley

2 teaspoons fresh thyme

2 tablespoons
minced shallots

2 tablespoons
white wine vinegar

1 small garlic clove, peeled

½ cup canola oil

½ cup olive oil

Salt and pepper

1. Drizzle a touch of olive oil into a nonstick pan on high heat. Place the lemons cut side down in the pan and sear for 2 minutes without moving. Remove lemons. Take out the seeds with a fork, and then, using your hands, squeeze out their juice into a blender. Discard lemons.

2. Add mustard, parsley, thyme, shallots, white wine vinegar and garlic to the lemon juice in the blender. Season with salt and pepper, then add canola and extra virgin olive oils. Blend on high until fully emulsified. Store in a mason jar for later use.

FABIO SAYS

Compound butters add great flavor to food, almost always at the end of cooking. I like to say these tempting butters are the final sprint to good flavor and a way to add an explosive punch without much effort. When you use compound butters, you get the luxury of butter without eating too much of it.

Clearly, I'm a big fan and I almost always have a few compound butters in the freezer, usually rolled into a log so that I can slice off what I need. I also store compound butters in small tubs and refrigerate or freeze them.

When I make them, they are about 50 percent butter and 50 percent other ingredients such as fresh herbs, citrus, garlic, chopped olives, grated or crumbled cheese, capers and black pepper. My rule of thumb is that the butter should look the color of the added ingredients. If there are a lot of herbs, the butter should be green; if there are black olives, the butter should be dark.

I start with softened, unsalted butter, softer than room temperature but never melting or melted. The best way to achieve this luscious texture is to leave the butter on the counter for a few hours. When you're in a hurry, you can soften it in the microwave, but if you do, take great care that it does not melt. When I can spear the butter with my finger and go all the way through to the counter, the butter is ready. Once the flavoring ingredients and butter are mixed, let it sit at room temperature for a few hours to allow the flavors to mingle. It's now ready to use or to refrigerate or freeze.

As I said, I usually add compound butters to dishes near the end of cooking—but not always. You can use them to sear fish, which cooks quickly. (If you use them in recipes with longer cooking times you run the risk of burning the herbs, lemon zest, capers or whatever else is in the butter.) Add some near the end of cooking to sautés, stews, sauces and soups. Put a pat on top of grilled steak or roasted vegetables. Spread it on crispy toast to eat alongside a glass of wine.

Parsley, Caper, Roasted Garlic and Shallot Butter

Yields ¾ cup

10 MINUTES PREP TIME
15 MINUTES COOKING TIME

3 shallots, sliced thin

¼ cup capers, rinsed

10 roasted garlic cloves,
see recipe p. 255

4 teaspoons grated
lemon zest

8 tablespoons
softened butter

¼ cup minced fresh parsley

Salt and pepper

Olive oil

1. Drizzle a touch of olive oil into a large nonstick pan on medium heat. Add the shallots and caramelize for 10 minutes. Add the capers and garlic cloves and cook for another 2 minutes. Season with salt and pepper, then remove from heat and cool completely on a plate.

2. Place cooled mixture into a stand mixer with paddle attachment, and add the lemon zest, butter and parsley. Beat until fully combined and adjust seasoning with salt and pepper to taste.

FABIO SAYS

I often make three or four of the **compound butters** you'll find on these pages, roll them into logs, and then freeze the butters for a few months. They're there when you need them.

Dill, Tarragon and Lemon Butter

**Yields 18 tablespoons
or a little more
than 2 sticks**

5-10 MINUTES PREP TIME

3 tablespoons chopped
fresh Italian parsley

4 tablespoons chopped
fresh dill

4 tablespoons chopped
fresh tarragon

1 clove garlic, minced

Juice of 1 lemon

2 sticks softened butter

Zest of 3 lemons

Salt and pepper

In a stand mixer with the paddle attachment, combine the parsley, dill, tarragon, garlic, lemon juice, butter, and lemon zest. Season with salt and pepper and beat butter until light and airy, about 2 minutes on medium speed.

Roasted Garlic, Thyme and Rosemary Butter

Yields ¾ cup

10 MINUTES PREP TIME

1 tablespoon minced
fresh rosemary

2 tablespoons minced
fresh parsley

2 tablespoons minced
fresh thyme

8 tablespoons
softened butter

10 roasted garlic cloves,
see recipe p. 255

Salt and pepper

Place rosemary, parsley, thyme, butter and garlic in bowl of stand mixer with paddle attachment. Season with salt and pepper, then beat until fully combined.

Blue Cheese and Black Pepper Butter

**Yields about
18 tablespoons**

5 MINUTES PREP TIME

2 tablespoons brandy

2 tablespoons fresh cracked
black pepper

2 tablespoons
minced shallots

½ cup crumbled gorgonzola

2 sticks softened butter

Salt, to taste

Put the brandy, black pepper, shallots, gorgonzola, butter and salt into a stand mixer with paddle attachment and beat until well mixed.

Oregano and Grana Padano Butter

Yields 13 tablespoons

5 MINUTES PREP TIME

2 teaspoons minced
fresh Italian parsley

1 tablespoon minced fresh
oregano

6 tablespoons grated
Grana Padano cheese

8 tablespoons
softened butter

2 garlic cloves, minced

Salt and pepper

In a stand mixer, combine the parsley, oregano, Grana Padano, butter and garlic. Season with salt and pepper and beat together using a paddle attachment.

Roasted Garlic, Black Olive and Basil Butter

**Yields about
18 tablespoons**

5 MINUTES PREP TIME

¼ cup chopped chives

½ cup chopped basil

½ cup chopped
Kalamata olives

2 sticks softened butter

10 cloves roasted garlic,
see recipe p. 255

Salt and pepper

Combine chives, basil, olives, butter and garlic in a stand mixer with paddle attachment and blend completely until smooth, about 1 to 2 minutes. Season with salt and pepper.

FABIO SAYS

When your air-tight **containers** are not in use, they might develop unappealing odors, especially if the lid is snapped in place. To eliminate the problem, put a pinch of salt in the container. Don't forget to rinse out the container before using, particularly if you're storing something sweet.

Fabio's Focaccia

Making focaccia is easy, easy, easy. So many people spend too much money on bread when they could very easily bake their own with ten or fifteen minutes of prep. Making your own bread is like your first kiss: a big deal until you do it once. (Really? That's all it takes? Easy! Let's do it again!) Also, when you make your own bread, people think you're pretty cool. Once you have a loaf or two of home-baked bread in the freezer, you can serve it defrosted and slightly heated or use it to make your own croutons or crostini.

If you plan to freeze the focaccia, bake it for only fifteen to twenty minutes, at which time the bread will be partially baked. Let it cool and then wrap it in freezer-safe plastic wrap or a plastic bag. When you want to serve it, take it from the freezer and put it in a preheated oven to finish baking. You can let the bread defrost before baking or not. If not, cover the frozen loaf with foil while baking.

Serves 8–10

5 MINUTES PREP TIME
2 HOURS COOKING TIME

½ teaspoon sugar
1 ½ teaspoons active dry yeast
1 cup warm water
2 ½ cups all-purpose flour
½ teaspoon salt
½ cup bread flour
¼ cup dried oregano
Sea salt
Olive oil

1. In a stand mixer, dissolve the sugar and yeast in the water. Add ¼ cup of the all-purpose flour and mix with the paddle attachment to incorporate. Let it rest for 1 minute.

2. Add the salt and bread flour. Add the rest of the all-purpose flour and mix until the dough pulls from the side.

3. Turn the dough out onto a lightly floured counter and knead it, adding more flour if needed until the dough forms a smooth ball. Place the dough in a large, oiled glass bowl and turn the dough to coat lightly with the oil.

4. Cover the bowl with plastic wrap. Let dough rise for around 1 hour, or until doubled in size. Once the dough has doubled in size, punch it and turn it out onto a lightly floured counter again. Stretch the dough into a 14-inch oval and place on a lightly oiled baking sheet.

5. Preheat the oven to 425°F. Let the dough rise again, uncovered, for 25 to 30 minutes. Sprinkle with sea salt and dried oregano, then dimple with your fingers.

6. Place focaccia inside the oven and bake for approximately 25 minutes, or until lightly browned.

Roasted Rosemary and Sage Croutons

Yields 4 cups croutons

10 MINUTES PREP TIME
15 MINUTES COOKING TIME

1 tablespoon fresh torn rosemary

1 tablespoon fresh torn sage

2 tablespoons melted butter

3 tablespoons olive oil

¼ cup torn parsley

½ cup grated Grana Padano cheese

4 cups medium-diced (½-inch) day-old sourdough or focaccia bread

2 garlic cloves, minced

Salt and pepper

1. Adjust oven rack to middle position and heat oven to 350°F.

2. In a large bowl, toss the rosemary, sage, butter, olive oil, parsley, Grana Padano, bread and garlic together. Adjust seasoning with salt and pepper.

3. Spread the bread cubes onto a baking sheet and bake until golden brown, about 15 minutes.

Zesty Orange and Calabrian Pepper Sauce

I love the sweet sharpness of Calabria chilies, and when blended with orange juice they turn into a sauce that you'll want to toss with cold chicken, drizzle over grilled fish or red meat, and use with roasted or grilled vegetables. Just an all-around good sauce, but one with unexpected flavor points.

Yields about 2 cups

¼ cup rice wine vinegar

2 cups orange juice

2 oranges,
cut into thick rounds

4 Calabria peppers,
rough chopped

1 teaspoon cornstarch

1 teaspoon cold water

2 teaspoons salt

1. Place the rice wine vinegar, orange juice, oranges, and peppers in a sauce pot and bring to a boil on high heat. Monitor the heat so that the orange juice doesn't overflow.

2. Let sauce reduce at a boil for 6 minutes. While it is reducing, mix the cornstarch and water in a small bowl. Pour the cornstarch mixture into the sauce, reduce heat to medium, and cook for 1 more minute to allow it to thicken. Add salt and cook for another 30 seconds. Remove from heat, blend fully with an immersion blender, and serve.

Roasted Lemons

As far as I'm concerned, this is the only way to have citrus. Heat up a sauté pan, and when it's nice and hot, put the lemon halves in the pan, cut sides down, and cook until the cut sides turn dark brown, almost black. At this point they're caramelized and will smell a little like sweet tea. I like to squeeze them over fish, fried foods, salads and vegetables for a great shot of lemon that's not as pungent as raw lemons.

When I roast lemons, I always work with more than five and usually cut up twenty or thirty. I caramelize them in the broiler, juice them in my juicer, and then pour the juice into the squeeze bottle. Ready, set, go! I don't usually put olive oil in the pan, but you can—it cooks the lemons a little faster, and they won't stain the pan.

5 MINUTES PREP TIME
5 MINUTES COOK TIME

¼ cup olive oil

5 lemons,
cut in half widthwise

Kosher salt, if desired

1. Pour olive oil into a large nonstick sauté pan on high heat. Wait until just smoking, then place in lemons, cut-side down. Without moving them, cook for 3 to 4 minutes, adjusting the heat slightly if pan starts to smoke too much.

2. Remove and cool on a plate. Season with a touch of salt, if desired.

Roasted Garlic

This is a shortcut version of how we roast garlic in the restaurant, but the principle is the same. There we peel hundreds of cloves and put them in a large cauldron. We then pour in enough olive oil to barely cover them. Next we roast them in a hot 400°F oven for five minutes and then turn off the heat and let the cloves sit in the hot oven in the hot oil as both cool. During this time, the cloves soften.

At home, I suggest you roast the garlic on your stovetop. Take apart three or four heads to come up with two cups of peeled, whole cloves (there are about twelve cloves in a head, and the count does not have to be exact here). Peel the cloves, put them in a deep pot, and then add olive oil just to cover. I have to say, peeling the cloves is the hardest part of the whole thing. Bring the oil to a boil over high heat and let it boil for one minute. After that minute, turn off the heat and let the cloves cool and soften in the oil. (*Tip:* Put the pot on a back burner. The oil is hot and by keeping the pot away from the front of the stove, you'll reduce the chance of an accident.)

If you want to flavor the oil, drop lemon zest, rosemary, thyme or sage—or anything else you fancy—into the oil before you add the garlic and before it's heated.

Once they're cool, the garlic cloves will look like perfect whole cloves, but if you press them gently, they go to mush. They taste milder and sweeter than raw garlic and can be used anywhere you want the pungency of garlic: eggs, sandwiches, toast, soups, sauces, Caesar dressing, dips and on and on.

Yields about 2 ½ cups

2 ½ cups olive oil
2 cups peeled garlic cloves

In a stockpot, add the garlic and olive oil. Bring to a boil and cook for one minute. Turn off the heat and let garlic cool completely in the oil. Store in an airtight container, keep refrigerated, and use within 3 weeks.

FABIO SAYS

Fresh, raw garlic must be used as soon as the clove is peeled. Even when it's still covered in papery skin and part of the head, the garlic goes bad really fast. Roasting garlic is an excellent way to extend its life and store it. Keep it in the fridge in a glass jar, covered with a little olive oil. The oil will solidify but the cloves will retain their irresistible flavor for up to a month. Best of all, they're ready when you are.

Roasted Mushroom Red Wine Sauce

Serves 4

10 MINUTES PREP TIME
10 MINUTES COOK TIME

½ cup olive oil

2 pounds assorted mushrooms, such as cremini, oyster, shiitake, and button

2 fresh rosemary sprigs

4 fresh thyme sprigs

½ cup Chianti or similar red wine

¼ cup chicken stock

2 tablespoons butter

Salt and pepper

1. Place a clean skillet over medium heat. Add the oil and mushrooms, then season with salt and pepper.

2. Add rosemary and thyme, and cook for 10 minutes, stirring occasionally.

3. Add the red wine, stirring to scrape up any cooking bits, and then add stock.

4. Let the liquid cook down by half and then take it off the heat. Stir in butter. Adjust seasoning with salt and pepper.

FABIO SAYS

I confess my own grandfather foraged for porcini mushrooms every fall, and guess who went with him? When the first early autumn rain fell, I knew I'd be up at 4 a.m. so we could make it to the woods as dawn broke. After a while, we'd have enough mushrooms—maybe ten pounds or so—to sell for a couple hundred dollars. Grandpa was so adept at finding porcinis that we'd fill the trunk of the car before we returned home—tired, wet, and hungry, and with some money in our pockets. But, as I said earlier, these days I stick with farm-grown.

INDEX

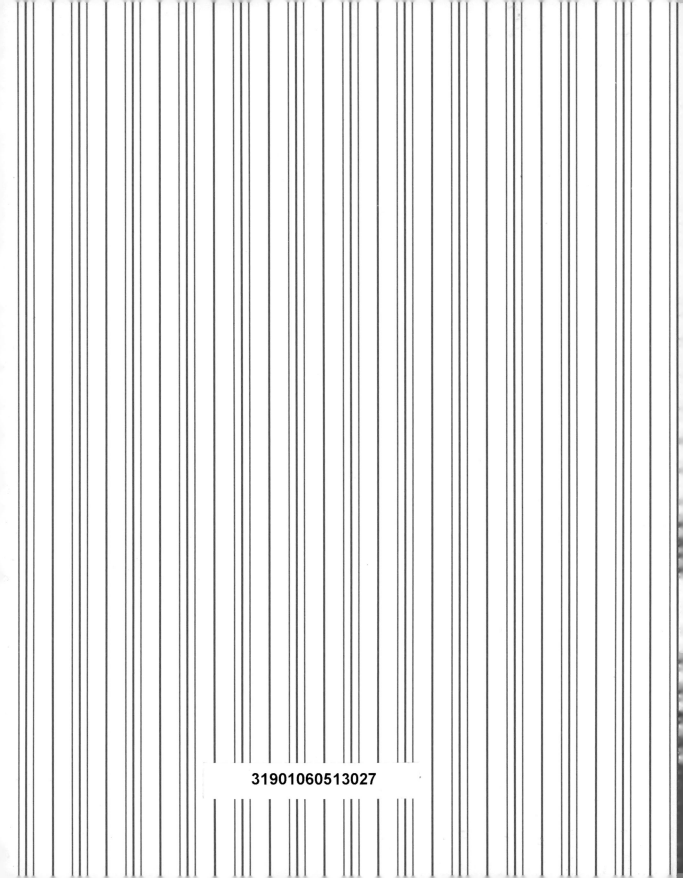

31901060513027